YOU ARE THE
PURPOSE

Unlock the Answers Within Yourself...

K. C. CATLIN

For Lily, a beautiful, free-spirit:

"Always remember that you are unique,

amazing & 100% LOVED!"

Mum xxx

Special Thanks

To my amazing parents, family, friends & soul companions
who have supported me on my "journey".

To the mentors & coaches who inspired me to take action
and whose wisdom provided the insights & stepping stones
along the way.

To the "teachers in disguise" who, unknowingly, provided
big AHA's and opportunities for personal growth.

My heart is full.

x

YOU ARE THE PURPOSE

Your purpose is not something outside of you...

YOU ARE the PURPOSE, even if you feel LOST at times

You see...

Your primary purpose is to be here on this learning journey

It is your purpose to forget your free spirit essence

It is your purpose to forget who you really are

It is your purpose to forget why you are here

It is your purpose to feel LOST

It is your purpose to question your existence

It is your purpose to find answers

It is your purpose to wake up

It is your purpose to let go of your "limiting story"

It is your purpose to free yourself

Your purpose is to discover how magical & significant you are

Your purpose is to step back into your power

Your purpose is to become your authentic self

Your purpose is to discover your passion and gifts

Your purpose is to live your highest potential and PURPOSE

OVERVIEW

This book is for you if you want to understand yourself better.

If you are searching for answers on how to feel happier in yourself & find more meaning in your life.

Maybe you feel lost in one or more areas of your life. Perhaps you are new to self-discovery, or maybe you have been on the path of personal growth and searching for your highest purpose for some time.

This book can help you unlock the answers within yourself and discover:

1. WHY you may feel LOST.
2. WHO you really are...
3. WHY you are experiencing unwanted patterns or negative emotions...
4. WHAT you can shift to FEEL BETTER...
5. WHEN you were programmed and conditioned.
6. HOW a step-by-step process can help you become the best, most authentic version of yourself. So, you can step into your power and live your highest potential & PURPOSE.

Index

PART I: Waking Up

1 Lost. 1

2 Who You Really Are. 17

3 Why it is Your Purpose to Forget 21

4 What Your Negative Emotions Mean. . . 27

5 How to Feel Better NOW. 33

6 What Limits You & Why. 41

PART II: Understanding Your Early Conditioning

7 Stage One – Safety. 51

8 Stage Two – Love & Connection 55

9 Stage Three – Self-worth. 59

10 Stage Four – Significance. 63

11 Stage Five – Power. 67

12 Stage Six – Abundance 71

13 Stage Seven – Freedom. 75

PART III: Finding the Answers Within Yourself

14 F.L.O.W. to Freedom Process. 83

15 Step 1: FIND OUT: What Limits You. 95

16 Step 2: LET GO: What Limits You. 101

17 Step 3: OPEN UP: Positive Expectation. . . .107

18 Step 4: WELCOME IN: New Possibilities . . .111

PART IV: Stepping into Your Power

19 Understanding The Law of Attraction. 117

20 Co-creating With the Universe 127

21 Understanding Your Power 137

22 Discovering Your Authentic Self. 147

PART V: The Journey & Keys to Success

23 The Journey to Your Highest Purpose. 155

24 KEY ONE: Celebration & Commitment. . . . 161

25 KEY TWO: Curiosity & Consistency. 171

26 KEY THREE: Community & Connection 177

27 KEY FOUR: Clarity & Confidence. 187

PART 1

WAKING UP

CHAPTER 1
LOST

"Hey, you!

"ME?!?"

Yes, YOU, are you OK?

I don't know...

I think I am lost...

I don't know why I am here...

I don't know what's the point of all this....

Oh, Kiddo, you can't be completely LOST.

After all, you are still HERE.

Would you like to figure out what's the matter?

Fancy telling me what it feels like to be LOST?

Oh, it feels icky and uncomfortable

I feel unsure and alone

I feel sad, like a nobody

Sometimes, I feel scared and worried

I can also feel frustrated and angry

I really don't understand myself or

why I feel the way I feel...

That sounds indeed a very uncomfortable place to be in...

Have you felt like this for some time?

Yes, I have felt like this for some time, and it happens more often these days... I can never tell when it will happen next and how long it will last.

Sometimes, I am more optimistic and want to get going, but something is holding me back – then I feel lost AND STUCK!

I have been trying to figure this out for some time...

So, you are saying you feel negative emotions and are stuck?

Yes, that's right... I feel like I go around in circles, and nothing ever changes. It's the same old "same-old".

I have no clue how I could change that.

So, are you saying you feel unhappy where you are and want things to change, but you need more clarity and direction? Do you at least know what you want to achieve?

Do you mean, apart from what I am doing at the moment?

I had a few ideas in the past, but nothing ever came of them, or they turned out not to be good ideas. I guess I always got stuck and didn't quite get there...

So, would you say that there are repeating patterns that are preventing you from achieving them?

I guess so. I get started, and then it doesn't work out. I am not sure what I am doing wrong. I am unsure if my ideas are wrong or something is wrong with ME. Whatever I have tried to change has not helped. I always end up back at square one.

Right, that sounds quite tiring...

Yes, it makes me want to give up and stop trying.

Do you feel you are getting enough support to achieve your ideas?

I can't say that I do. I have learned that most people are only interested in their own stuff.

OK, it seems you are indeed LOST, but not quite as you think.

Not quite as I think?

Yes! Do you realise that there is

ABSOLUTELY NOTHING WRONG WITH YOU? You are just

Looping On the Search Treadmill

I am looping on the search treadmill?

Yes, that's what LOST stands for…

But what does it mean?

It means you are searching for something; you are taking steps; you are putting in the effort, and it looks like you are moving in the right direction, BUT you are not getting where you want to go.

Like on a treadmill?

Yes, like on a treadmill… You can see the goal ahead, but you are not getting any nearer. You like an idea and try to move towards it, BUT it doesn't work. Next time, you might try to run faster, but it only exhausts you more. So, you give up on that idea. Then you see something else, and this

7

time, you might take the slow and steady approach, but you still can't get there.

Because I am on a treadmill...

Yes, because you are on a treadmill and because you are searching for things outside of you. You think when you can get over there or achieve this goal, you will feel happier.

But I am sure I would...

Yes, I am sure you would, but for how long...

Honestly, have you never achieved any of your ideas?

Well, thinking of it now...

I may have on a few occasions.

What happened when you achieved them? Did you soon get bored and chase after the next idea...

I guess I DID...

So, would you say the search continued to find the next thing and the next thing to make you feel better?

Hmmm... you have a point, but isn't that what most people do?

Yes, if you mean all the people who are chasing dreams and feeling unhappy, stressed, and exhausted. There are plenty of those around, that's for sure...

I don't know if I understand...

I guess I am saying that just because many people are doing the same silly thing, it doesn't mean it works.

So, are you saying everyone unhappy, stressed, and exhausted is LOST and looping on the search treadmill?

Yes, possibly, but like you, they don't know they are looping. It can take a long time to realise that something is not working. Some collapse through sheer burnout or exhaustion. Others like you had enough and are ready to give up...

But it's hard, isn't it? There is something inside of you that is still searching for something.

Yes, you are right, but what is that?

You are searching indeed for something, but it's not something outside of you, like a better job. It is NOT the perfect relationship, more money, a luxury car, the next holiday, sports trophies, fame or glamour. They might be great things to have, but they don't fulfil us.

But I am sure I would feel happy having them...

Yes, I don't doubt they would make you happy for a while – that's why I said they won't fulfil you.

What's the difference?

You can have all the stuff in the world, even outstanding success, but you can still feel unfulfilled, empty and alone inside...

What you are truly searching for is fulfilment, joy, and inner happiness.

Inner happiness?

Yes, the happiness and inner freedom you feel when you have found yourself.

When I found myself?

Yes, you feel lost because you are searching for YOURSELF and your PURPOSE.

I am searching for myself and my purpose?

Yes, you are searching for answers to explain:

Who you really are? Why you are here? The meaning of your life and existence.

Woah...I am searching for the meaning of my life and existence... Are you sure?

Yes, I am pretty sure!

OK, let me ask you A VERY IMPORTANT QUESTION:

Do you remember you are here for a reason and that you are significant & powerful?

What the hell are you talking about?

Me? Powerful & significant?

I take that as a NO...

No!

Why would I think that I am powerful or significant?

Because you ARE!

It indeed sounds like you are slightly lost...

But don't worry; this is all part of your reason for being here and part of your purpose...

What nonsense are you talking about NOW?

Feeling LOST is part of my purpose for being here?

Trust me, I know because I was once where you are right now, and I have discovered that being lost and stuck on this treadmill is part of the plan and our purpose...

Would you like some help to understand:

WHO YOU ARE?

And why you feel this way?

Really? YOU, too, were stuck on the treadmill?

You seem happy and joyful to me!

Yes, I might seem happy and joyful NOW, but believe me,

I can relate to where you are now.

Yes, please, I want to understand myself,

and right now, I would try anything to feel better.

Not too long ago, I was feeling really down...

People or situations often triggered me.

My mood kept changing rapidly.

I could feel annoyed, frustrated, or angry quite quickly.

I had doubts and fears that stopped me from doing things.

I tried to control it, but eventually realised I had ZERO control over the outside world that triggered me...

Sounds familiar?

Yep!

That sounds very much like me...

The more I try to control the situation, the more frustrated or anxious I become...

The more I think about it, the worse I feel...

It seems hopeless.

So, tell me, what happened?

After going round and round looping on the treadmill, not knowing WHY I felt the way I felt, why I had triggers and what created the patterns that kept me stuck. I started asking different questions, and guess what?

I got different answers...

This changed EVERYTHING for me!

What?!

You just started asking different questions?

How would that help?

Before, I was asking myself disempowering questions like...

Why do I feel so worried?

Why are people so unsupportive?

Why is this happening to me?

They seem pretty reasonable questions to me...

Why would they be the problem?

Because these questions were focused on the problem rather than the solution, and we cannot find the answers when we are focused on the problem. Instead, it keeps us on the search treadmill, and we stay STUCK with the problem and potentially make it bigger.

Really?!?

I never knew that...

I thought that by focusing on a problem, we could solve it.

This might be true for a mathematical equation or a project that needs planning. But this isn't true when it comes to our emotions.

When we focus on our negative emotions, we feel more of them. When we focus on what goes wrong, we will spot more things that go wrong.

This is called "The Universal Law of Attraction"; we get more of what we pay attention to, even if it's unwanted!

I can explain more about how this works later...

OK, so you started asking different questions? How did this change things?

I started looking inside of me to understand myself and what caused my negative emotions, patterns, and triggers.

And what did you discover?

I discovered that it's not something outside of us – it is because we have LOST ourselves and because we have totally forgotten WHO we are.

Are you saying that the ONLY reason we feel negative emotions, feel triggered, and have unwanted patterns is because we have forgotten WHO we are?

How can there be only ONE reason when so many things can trigger us and make us feel unhappy?

I know it's tricky to understand at first, but bear with me…

You think of many reasons because you are searching AGAIN for a reason in the outside world. However, these are all the things you cannot control, and you won't find the solution there.

It becomes much easier when you focus on the ONE thing you can control… and that is YOU and why you feel this way.

OK, so you are telling me THE ONLY reason these things are happening is because I have forgotten who I am, and I have lost myself? Like some kind of amnesia?

I can't believe THIS; this sounds like a very random concept…

Well, not only have you forgotten who you are…

On top of it, you were also programmed as soon as you came here to earth, which adds to the problem.

Yeah RIGHT!!!

How on earth would we have been programmed?!?!?

I think you are a bit MAD...

I understand your doubts, but please hear me out if you want to find a real solution to your problem...

You said that you don't know who you are and don't seem to have control over your unwanted patterns, triggers, or negative emotions, right?

I guess...

So, wouldn't it be better if the solution was connected to YOU and your amnesia & programming?

Because IF the problem is within you and not outside of you, you have a better chance of FIXING IT.

Hmmm...

As reluctant as I am (and hate to admit it), you might have a point!

If the problem is that I don't know who I am and have been what you call "programmed", maybe I can find a way to un-program myself...

I might as well hear if you have any solution up your sleeve for this.

Excellent, I was hoping you would say that...

It shows you want to create a change and find a solution.

The good news is that I indeed have what you call a "solution up my sleeve" that can help you to un-program what needs to be un-programmed for you to feel better...

But before I share this with you, I want you to understand WHO you really are & HOW you have been programmed.

CHAPTER 2
WHO YOU REALLY ARE

OK, this is getting interesting now...

tell me who I am and how I have been programmed?

Sure, so who are you?

It might help if you understand that we all have things in common but are also very different.

All of us here on earth have come here for a learning experience, an opportunity to grow and expand. We are all more than this physical body – this is just our avatar for this lifetime. Our avatar is our body and personality and is unique every time we come to Earth. But the part of us that comes here to learn and grow stays the same. Some call this part our SOUL, core self, higher self, life force energy, or GOD.

You are a free Spirit.

This is who YOU really are...

"WOA... WHAT?!

Our body is just an avatar?

Which we change every time we come to earth?

Are you completely bonkers?

Like in reincarnation or something?

That's right, we are spiritual beings having a human experience, and we chose to come here...

Some believe we choose the family we are born into for a specific experience. We choose a particular environment where we get another chance to complete a learning that had not been completed in a previous life.

You mean, we really come here for a reason?

Yes, that's right, and that core spirit self KNOWS the reason and remembers its eternal, divine nature. The trouble is that our avatars have no idea.

And what is that eternal and divine nature?

We are vibrational beings of pure positive energy, light & love at the core level, and we have come here to shine this love and light into the world.

Our core self knows with 100% certainty SEVEN CORE TRUTHS about itself...

The Seven CORE TRUTHS? What are they?

Your Seven Core Truths are:

1: YOU ARE 100% **SAFE**

2: YOU ARE 100% **LOVED & CONNECTED**

3: YOU ARE 100% **WORTHY**

4: YOU ARE 100% **SIGNIFICANT**

5: YOU ARE 100% **POWERFUL**

6: YOU ARE 100% **ABUNDANT**

7: YOU ARE 100% **FREE**

Really?

Yes, because you are connected to pure consciousness and everything out there in this universe.

I am connected to the universe?

Bloody Hell!!! This is a lot to take in...

YES! Your core self is in constant connection with the universe...

And this is the part of YOU that has all YOUR answers.

You see...They are right when they say:

"We have all the answers within ourselves".

This is the part of you that knows YOUR best path to your highest purpose.

So why don't I remember this?

Why don't I know why I am here or what my purpose is?

CHAPTER 3

WHY IT IS YOUR PURPOSE TO FORGET

You don't remember because it is part of the plan to forget.

It is also part of the plan that you become programmed and conditioned and feel lost... Because your purpose is to learn, rediscover and remember who you really are at the core AND this avatar in this lifetime. While the core remains the same, the avatar is new. Your avatar will, most likely, have completely different character traits, strengths, weaknesses, values, likes, and dislikes from your last avatar. In addition, it undergoes its unique programming.

Your avatar is programmed and does not know about its core self, but it gets feedback in the form of emotions. Every time we are triggered or feel negative emotions, it is because of the different beliefs and opinions between our human avatar and our core.

So, are you saying I have negative emotions, patterns, and triggers because I have been programmed?

How come I don't remember anything?

That's because a major part of our programming is subconscious and occurs in the first seven years of our lives. It starts when we are a foetus in our mother's womb. Everything she experiences becomes programmed in us in preparation for the outside world...

I didn't know this...how does this affect us?

Well... depending on how safe, loved, and supported our mother felt during pregnancy, we expect to be safe and nurtured when we are born...

If our mother experienced trauma, stress, or fears during pregnancy, we also carry this programming! As a result, we might be prone to feeling scared and anxious.

Wow- so we can feel anxious because our mother felt scared when she was pregnant with us?

That IS SCARY and a bit bonkers...

Yes, a lot of our early programming isn't even ours and is extra powerful because it is the first programming we undergo, AND it doesn't stop there...

Then, of course, everything that happens at birth and in early childhood programs us further. We are like sponges that absorb everything without a filter. It all goes straight into the subconscious, and we don't even know it's there!

Oh my, oh my...

Do you mean everything that happened to us programs us in this way?

What effects does this have?

I am glad you ask...

It creates fears & limiting beliefs we have about ourselves, and those limiting beliefs oppose what our CORE authentic self knows to be true.

Limiting beliefs like we are not safe, not loved, not worthy, and not significant.

What's more, it creates layers upon layers of conditioning that cover up the knowledge of our CORE authentic self.

So, are you saying we are like ONIONS... with layers and layers of conditioning and our core self, who knows we are safe and good enough gets covered up?

Is this how we forget who we are?

Yes, you are spot on...

Our Core authentic self still exists under all the layers of our conditioned outer self.

Whenever our Avatar's CONDITIONED BELIEFS clash with our CORE TRUTHS, we feel negative emotions or get triggered.

Likewise, if our Avatar's beliefs are in harmony with our core truths, we feel positive emotions, and all is good.

This gives you an idea of why you feel certain emotions.

This is super interesting. Could you please give me some more examples?

Layers of
Conditioning

Core self

CHAPTER 4

WHAT YOUR NEGATIVE EMOTIONS MEAN

Of course! Let's take the seven core truths and contradicting, conditioned beliefs to understand how our negative emotions are created.

LONELINESS

Loneliness is experienced when your human self believes it is alone. Still, your core self knows it is connected to everything and everyone, including the universe, and doesn't feel alone.

DOUBT

You experience doubt when you believe you are not good enough, but your core self knows you are totally worthy, deserving & good enough, and there is no need to prove yourself.

WORRY

Worry is experienced when you fear that you are insignificant, but your core self knows you are unique and special. You are a miracle simply by having made it here to earth.

ANXIETY

You may experience anxiety when you feel powerless because you are unaware of the power that your core self knows you carry deep within yourself.

LACK

You experience lack when you feel there is something missing. This could be a lack of time, money, or opportunities. This tends to happen when your lost self is focused on scarcity rather than the abundance your core self knows is available and also knows your power to attract and manifest it.

TRAPPED

You can feel trapped, stuck, and left without a choice when you have forgotten that you are a free spirit and have a choice in everything.

FEAR

Fear is created when your core self knows you are safe, but your human self feels vulnerable - for example, during public speaking because of fear of being judged or fear of messing up. Of course, there is "real fear" that can prevent us from danger, but most of our modern-day fears are not life-threatening. Your core self doesn't even fear death because it knows it is eternal by nature.

I see… Thank you!

This is quite eye-opening when you put it like this!

So, our emotions show if our beliefs match or disagree.

Precisely, your emotions tell you exactly how aligned or out of alignment you are between your human beliefs and those of your core self.

If you feel happy, joyful, and excited, you know you are on the right track with your thoughts and beliefs.

You can also understand your emotions in terms of energy, vibrations, and frequency. Think of them as HIGH & LOW. That's where the casual terms High and Low vibes come from.

Here is a model of the emotional scale that explains the emotions in a visual representation.

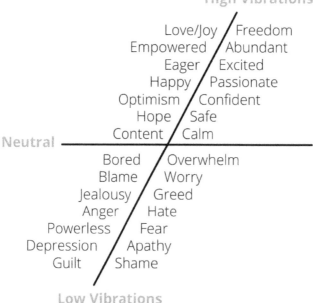

The Emotional Scale

High Vibrations

Love/Joy / Freedom
Empowered / Abundant
Eager / Excited
Happy / Passionate
Optimism / Confident
Hope / Safe
Content / Calm

Neutral

Bored / Overwhelm
Blame / Worry
Jealousy / Greed
Anger / Hate
Powerless / Fear
Depression / Apathy
Guilt / Shame

Low Vibrations

Some of the highest energy emotions are love, freedom, and appreciation.

Some of the lowest, slowest emotions in terms of frequency are shame, guilt, and fear. More neutral emotions are boredom and calm.

Can you give me some examples?

Of course, think of a person who feels depressed; their energy is low and slow and often, they struggle to even get out of bed. Then, in contrast, think of someone happy or excited about something. Their energy tends to be high.

The more time you spend in the top part of the emotional scale, the higher your energy is. You feel good and are less likely to feel triggered because your batteries are recharged.

The more time you spend in low emotions, the worse you feel because your batteries don't recharge, and you get triggered much easier.

The good news is that when you start feeling triggered or experience negative emotions, you can do something straight away.

What would that be?

When you feel negative emotions or triggered, you can do one of three things to feel better...

Tell me, what are the three things that I can do?

CHAPTER 5

HOW TO FEEL BETTER NOW

1.   SHIFT YOUR THOUGHTS

Become mindful and aware of the thoughts that are going through your head. Most people don't observe their automatic thoughts or question them. This chatter of your inner voice can be like a running commentary. It will assess everything you observe in your environment. It will judge and categorise everything into opportunities or threats and likes or dislikes. The problem with that is that we are often unaware that it focuses on the negative rather than the positive. So, it will predominantly focus on things that go wrong rather than well. If it's a limiting thought, you will experience negative emotions.

However, if you can find the thought that caused the negative emotion, you can try substituting it for a better feeling thought.

For example, you feel frustrated because your partner has AGAIN left the milk out of the fridge. Your thought might be that "they are so inconsiderate". It's an automatic thought, but it will leave you feeling unhappy about the situation. When you recognise that this thought creates a feeling of disappointment or unhappiness, you can step in.

So instead of thinking "they are inconsiderate", you could consciously replace it with a thought like: "They are swamped right now and probably just forgot." This creates a more neutral feeling.

Mindful thought changes are a great way to improve how you feel. It takes a little practice, but once you get the hang of it becomes easier and eventually automatic.

So, some thoughts feel better, and others feel worse?

What if you cannot find a better or good feeling thought?

You can try tip number two....

2. SHIFT YOUR FOCUS

If you cannot replace the thought and are struggling to find anything more positive to think about, then…

STOP THINKING ABOUT IT!!!

This is maybe easier said than done, but really…

If something feels quite triggering or negative, sometimes it is best to think about something completely different or unrelated. Look the other way; distract yourself by putting on your favourite song, for example. Remember, only thinking about the problem won't solve it but perpetuates it.

Do you mean I should ignore it?

Yes, that's right. Look out there. So many people are so focused on everything that goes wrong. The news and the media also feed chaos, drama, wars, and conflicts. When we focus on everything that goes wrong, we feel worse and worse.

Are you saying I shouldn't watch the news?

I am saying that you have a choice in what you consume. Become mindful of how it makes you feel. The information you consume is like the food you eat. If you eat healthy and nutritious food, you give your body the best conditions to function well. What you focus on with your mind is the food for your emotions.

You can choose what you look at, listen to, and read. You can focus more on what makes you feel good and less on what makes you worried or unhappy.

Do you mean like the News? They definitely make me feel terrible… Is this what you are doing?

Yes, I deliberately stopped watching or reading things that don't make me feel good many years ago, and I have been feeling happier and lighter ever since…

Maybe I should give this a go?

Maybe you should if you care how you feel and want to test it for yourself.

And then there is the third option…

OK, so what is the third option?

3. SHIFT YOUR LIMITING BELIEFS

The third option is to align with your seven core truths by letting go of the limiting beliefs that are the root cause of your negative emotions and triggers.

You can remove the triggers by letting go of the limiting beliefs.

When you remove the triggers, you remove the reason for your unwanted pattern and negative emotions.

But HOW do we do that?

How can we peel back the ONION Layers?

How can we un-condition ourselves?

The simple answer is bit by bit.

Layer by layer, whenever something comes up...

Remember, your emotions tell you when you have hit a layer, a limiting belief, or a bit of unwanted programming.

That's when you can take action when you know how.

How can I re-program my limiting beliefs?

They are not proper layers I can touch...

You are right; they are not real onion layers.

To understand HOW you can re-program yourself, it is helpful to understand three other things:

WHEN & HOW we become programmed.

WHAT our limiting beliefs are.

WHERE they are stored.

Wow, I didn't think I would learn so much today...

My head is spinning a bit, to be honest...

But tell me WHEN & HOW I was programmed.

What are my limiting beliefs and programs, and where are they stored?

OK, let's start with the easiest one of the three....

CHAPTER 6
WHAT LIMITS YOU & WHY

OK, are you ready for this, Kiddo?

Yep, I am listening!

ALL of your thoughts and beliefs that you have EVER thought (all millions or billions) still exist as an energetic, holographic memory...

Sorry, A WHAT?!

Now, you've really got my head spinning...

What on earth is a holographic, energetic memory?

It just means it is a very detailed memory that contains all the information about WHAT happened, WHEN it happened, WHO was there, HOW it felt and more.

Oh...that's interesting...

So, where does this memory exist?

In MY HEAD, in my MIND?

No, it's not a thought in your mind or stored in the brain.

Because it's an "energetic memory," it is NOT part of your brain. It is stored in your electromagnetic field.

HANG ON NOW...

What's this electromagnetic field you are talking about?

Right. Remember I was telling you that we are vibrational electric beings... Now is probably a good time to tell you that every cell in your body produces energy, and you have different energy centres in the body.

Your heart is by far the most powerful one, creating a powerful electromagnetic field around you.

I AM NOT SURE I CAN TAKE MUCH MORE...

Why have I never heard of this?

Most likely because the electromagnetic field is invisible, and most people don't know they are made of energy. Also, it is not taught in school...yet!

This is a visual of your electromagnetic field. It extends invisibly around you. Sometimes, this field is also referred to as your AURA.

And what does it do?

This electromagnetic field has various functions, but I don't want to overload you. So, for NOW, just know that all your Holographic Energetic Memories are stored here like FILES.

Does this mean absolutely EVERYTHING that I have ever experienced is stored in this "electromagnetic field" like a GIANT COMPUTER?

Yes, CORRECT!!!

You've hit the nail on the head. "As they say."

You can imagine every memory like a "FILE" that gets stored with all the information on it...

Every time you experience a similar situation - a new FILE is created and added to the corresponding "LIMITING BELIEF FOLDER." This is how your subconscious classifies your experiences. It keeps memories of similar experiences together.

OK, understood – so all memories and experiences get classified into folders...

And then what happens?

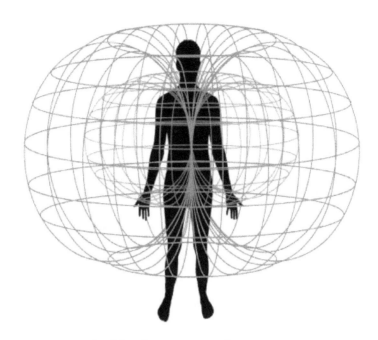

Nothing happens at all...

What do you mean, NOTHING HAPPENS AT ALL?!

Surely something must be happening...

You are, of course, RIGHT; something DOES happen... But it is so teeny-weeny and subtle that it almost goes completely unnoticed, and it's called...

"The accumulative effect!"

The accumulative effect?!

Yes, every time we experience a situation where we feel unsafe or disconnected, for example, it gets added to one or more folders. We accumulate or collect more and more memories of similar experiences, and they all add up — that's the accumulative effect.

And why is this important?

This explains why the older a limiting belief is, the more havoc or disruptions it can cause because we have added SOOO much stuff.

Imagine seven main files holding all your memories of similar limiting beliefs and fears. They could be pretty full by now, even if you are still young. All your childhood, teenage, and early adult memories are stored there.

Are there really only seven folders?

Of course, there are more folders for good and happy memories (your achievements, the joyful and happy times you have experienced), but for the sake of un-programming your limiting beliefs, we only focus on these seven for now.

Oh...OK, so what goes in which one?

To understand what the seven folders contain, it is good to know roughly at what age they may have been created.

Why is this important?

Because they correlate with the Seven conditioning stages of our younger self. Would you like to know how and why you may have become programmed?

Absolutely...

Great, so the Seven folders correlate to the Seven stages of our main subconscious programming, which happens roughly in the first seven years of our lives...

Why only roughly?

Roughly, because our life doesn't start when we are born. It begins in the womb, so the first stage starts there. Also, some of us develop quicker than others. We are all exposed to unique circumstances, so everyone's programming is unique, too. The examples I will share with you only focus on the typical challenges a child may face growing up interacting with the outside world. It deliberately DOES NOT take into account any uniquely challenging situations or circumstances because I want to highlight just HOW programmed we can become even if nothing out of the ordinary happens to us.

So, if what you are about to hear makes you think:

"Well, this is nothing compared to what I was exposed to". Please take a mental note of those events and feelings as they can help you later to un-program yourself.

The seven conditioning stages look at the following:

HOW
"aware" we are as a baby/child at each stage

THE CHALLENGES
we may encounter as we progress through this stage of childhood

WHAT
Key questions we ask ourselves

THE FEARS & LIMITING BELIEFS
we may conclude as a result

PART II

UNDERSTANDING YOUR
EARLY CONDITIONING

CHAPTER 7
STAGE ONE - SAFETY

Conditioning Stage 1

Womb to Birth

Key Questions:

Am I safe? Am I loved?

What environment am I being born into?

The Challenges:

The foetus has no filter and is one with the mother. Every fear and worry she experiences the baby experiences, too. Does she feel loved and supported in her relationship? How does she feel about the pregnancy? Is she nourishing herself well? Is the environment making her calm and relaxed or stressed and exhausted? Is she joyful & happy? All memories of our time in the womb and birth experience are stored in our subconscious.

Contains limiting beliefs & fears like

- I am not safe
- I am in danger
- I am scared I will get hurt
- I am vulnerable
- I am unprotected
- I am unwanted

The "I am NOT SAFE FOLDER" is probably the biggest one because it is the first created and will continually be added to. As our conscious awareness increases with age, so does our understanding of potential danger. How safe and supported we (our mother and us) feel will determine if and how much we trust.

CHAPTER 8

STAGE TWO -
LOVE & CONNECTION

Conditioning Stage 2

Age: Birth - 2

Key Questions:

Am I safe? Am I loved?

Am I nurtured?

The Challenges:

The biggest challenge is the sudden separation from our mother at birth. The outside world feels less safe than the womb. We are vulnerable and reliant on our mothers or caregivers. Are we receiving the nurturing we need to develop healthily? Are we receiving the love & affection we crave? Are we receiving the time & attention we require to thrive happily? Is our home environment safe? Is the environment harmonious and calm, or stressful and chaotic? Are the people surrounding us at ease or in conflict? Do we feel loved, connected, and bonded in our family? Or do we feel alone or neglected?

Contains limiting beliefs & fears like

- I am not loved/lovable
- I am not connected
- I don't belong
- I am alone
- I am unwanted
- Fear of abandonment

Our early childhood experiences influence the memories stored here. Our relationship with our mother, father and siblings and how nurtured, loved and connected we felt will determine our relationships in the future. Do we trust people? Do we feel we belong?

CHAPTER 9

STAGE THREE – SELF-WORTH

Conditioning Stage 3

Age: 2 - 3

Key Questions:

Am I safe? Am I loved?

Am I good enough?

The Challenges:

As we become more aware of the world around us, we begin to wonder how we fit in. A younger sibling may appear, and we suddenly get less attention from our mother and start seeking more recognition and approval from our father or other caregivers. We may question our place in the family structure. Are we as worthy & deserving of attention as our siblings? Maybe we start child daycare and are suddenly out of our comfort zone and feel challenged and fearful. Surrounded by other children, we begin to compare ourselves with others. We may ask ourselves, are we good enough?

Contains limiting beliefs & fears like

- I am not worthy
- I am not deserving
- I am not good enough
- Fear of being judged
- Fear of not fitting in
- Fear of separation

This highly influential folder gets established at a critical point in our lives when we are partially aware yet still innocent. Our 2-3-year-old self has not yet developed the ability to ask empowering questions, nor has our young brain "learned to reason." So, anytime we feel challenged or fearful and ask why we feel this way, our younger self may conclude it must be because we are "NOT GOOD ENOUGH!"

This is a limiting belief that most of us carry into adulthood and can negatively impact any area of our lives. It can show up as overgiving, lack of boundaries, self-doubt, fear, worries and procrastination.

CHAPTER 10
STAGE FOUR - SIGNIFICANCE

Conditioning Stage 4

Age: 3 - 4

Key Questions:

Am I safe? Am I loved?

Am I significant?

The Challenges:

We become more aware at this stage but still feel free and playful enough to imagine conquering the world as 3-4-year-old superheroes, princes and princesses because we like to feel significant and special. However, most of us start our formal education around this time, and suddenly, we are in the outside world for long periods surrounded by children of similar ages, who will tell us very directly if they like us or not. In addition, we are taught to conform as we learn to sit still and listen. This can be a harsh environment, and we can feel exposed to unkind comments that can leave us to conclude that we are nothing special.

Contains limiting beliefs & fears like

- I am insignificant
- I am not unique
- I am nothing special
- It is safer to fit in & be like everyone else
- Fear of being bullied
- Fear of being judged

We begin to compare ourselves with others and we can feel less and less SIGNIFICANT. We learn that being unique and special can draw unwanted attention and we can find ourselves in uncomfortable or challenging situations with the surrounding people. This can be the time when many opt for what feels like the safest option. We try to fit in order to avoid confrontations and negative emotions.

CHAPTER 11

STAGE FIVE - POWER

Conditioning Stage 5

Age: 4 - 5

Key Questions:

Am I safe? Am I loved?

Am I Powerful?

The Challenges:

Having learned that being in the dynamics of peers (where we may have felt criticised, judged or made fun of), we likely want to find a strategy to avoid confronting situations and negative emotions. We will probably adopt one of two strategies. We either become leaders who speak up and display power to avoid peer domination. Alternatively, we become more adaptive and less outspoken and opt for the quieter strategy to fit in. We further drop our uniqueness and try to be "just like" our peers with whom we want to be friends.

Contains limiting beliefs & fears like

- I am not powerful
- Fear of being bullied or judged
- Fear of not belonging
- Fear of speaking up & being seen
- Fear of being exposed & made fun of
- It is safer to fit in & be like everyone else
- I need to dominate

When you read the last point, you may wonder why this is in this folder. The "I need to dominate" belief is here because it is likely driven by an underlying fear of not being powerful or good enough. Some young children regarded as leaders may have only become so by being overly dominant to distract from their own insecurities.

CHAPTER 12
STAGE SIX - ABUNDANCE

Conditioning Stage 6

Age: 5 - 6

Key Questions:

Am I safe? Am I loved?

Am I abundant?

The Challenges:

Competitiveness is at a new high level now. With increasing age, we become more consciously aware of the world and how it functions. We experience things like time restrictions, i.e., being unable to play longer. We become attuned to the possessions we have. We learn how money is the means to get what we want. We learn about our family's lack or abundance of time, money, and love. And we also begin to understand our social status by comparison with others.

Contains limiting beliefs & fears like

- I am limited
- I can't
- There is not enough time
- There is not enough money
- There are limited opportunities
- Others have more XYZ
- Others have better XYZ

Comparing ourselves with others is natural, but it can create feelings of unfairness and jealousy when we realise how much "better off" other people are. The holidays, the happy family time, the house, the cars, the THINGS. It can also create anger and frustration when we realise our limitations and lack of opportunities and possibilities. These may just be the conclusions of a 6-year-old, but they can create limiting beliefs for a lifetime.

CHAPTER 12

STAGE SEVEN - FREEDOM

Conditioning Stage 7

Age: 6 – 7

Key Questions:

Am I safe? Am I loved?

Am I Free?

The Challenges:

With yet more awareness, we begin to realise how free or limited we are. Are we free to express ourselves and our individuality? Are we free to do what we want? Can we get the things we want? Can we get things to go our way? To see what's possible, we start to push boundaries in a more calculated way. We begin to see ourselves as autonomous individuals and fight for a new level of independence. With this, we experience our first major setbacks as we discover our limitations.

Contains limiting beliefs & fears like

- I am limited
- I can't
- I have no choice
- I am not allowed

The "I am not free Folder" includes so much more than just the belief to be limited because we can experience FREEDOM or the LACK of freedom on many levels. There is the inner freedom that creates our feelings of joy and happiness. The freedom of thought, choice, and free will. The freedom to express ourselves, the freedom of speech, the freedom to create, and the freedom to become anything we wish!

Every time we feel we "Can't," there is a belief that we are NOT FREE.

What Do you think?

Wow... I think my mind is well and truly blown...

I can see how we become conditioned and programmed. If we don't feel safe and loved, then we don't feel good enough, and then we don't feel significant. When we don't feel significant, we are in a bit of trouble...

Exactly... And what's more- when we don't feel significant or good enough, we won't grow to the next level. We need to feel good enough and have positive beliefs that support us. Only when we believe we are safe, secure, loved & supported, good enough and significant will we step up into our authentic power...

Ahh, is it like a ladder?

It's more like a pyramid that gives you a solid foundation, makes it much easier to climb to the top and helps you grow and achieve what you want to do. A ladder has no solid foundation and can be wobbly.

That's why you feel stuck and don't know what next steps to take because something (like an invisible force) is holding you back from getting up there.

Yes, this is how I feel...But why?

What is this invisible force?

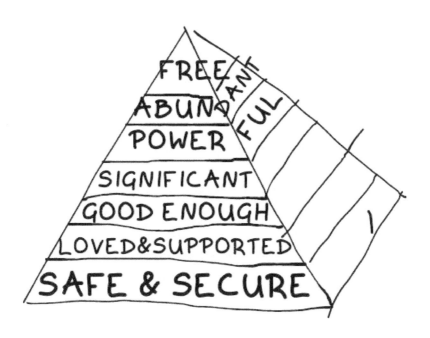

The force you feel is the resistant energy of your subconscious fears and limiting beliefs. It is like a magnet holding you back from stepping into your authentic POWER.

Even if you know where you want to go, you can't get there easily because it takes tremendous effort, creating pain if you have to push past your limiting beliefs and fears. You are stuck on that treadmill.

Yes, I can relate…Everything I tried felt like hard work, and I wasn't even sure if it was the right thing to do.

So, are my limiting beliefs standing in my way and holding me back?

Precisely, that's why it's a good idea to remove them altogether by un-programming them rather than trying to push past them.

Also, it is common to have no clarity when you are still programmed with all those limiting beliefs.

Only by removing the conditional layers will you get to know your true, authentic self. Only then will you truly understand your values, likes, and dislikes. And only when you experience life as your most authentic self will your highest purpose become apparent.

This can be very challenging even for people who have long known that they are here for a higher purpose to help and inspire others. They might have clarity on how they want to make a difference in the world, but they still struggle to free themselves and step into their authentic power.

What stops them from stepping into their true power and highest potential? Why is that?

Because every time they step out of their comfort zone or take on a new or unfamiliar bigger challenge, they are likely to hit another layer of fears and limiting beliefs.

It can be very daunting and scary to step out and be visible. It can feel overwhelming and unsafe if you haven't got the right support and guidance on how to free yourself from those limiting beliefs.

So, what's the answer? What's the solution? How can we free ourselves?

PART III
FINDING THE ANSWERS
WITHIN YOURSELF

CHAPTER 14

F.L.O.W. TO FREEDOM PROCESS

So, you would like to learn how to free yourself from unwanted programming and these limiting beliefs?

Hell YES...

OK, so there is a four-step process I call:

F.L.O.W. to Freedom

Step 1:

F = FIND OUT what is limiting you

Step 2:

L = LET GO what is limiting you

Step 3:

O = OPEN UP to positive expectation

Step 4:

W = WELCOME IN new possibilities

But HOW the heck do we do this?

OK, let me go into more detail about each of the four steps. To get to the bottom of our negative emotional patterns, we want to become detectives and find out what's happening. Because everyone is uniquely programmed, and we don't get a manual or instructions telling us what is going on…

Is that why I feel so lost?

None of the advice I've tried helped or only made a small difference…

Of course, NOT…

because they don't have YOUR ANSWERS

Only you have the answers to yourself, and I only have the answers to myself.

But by using the 4 F.L.O.W. steps,

YOU CAN find YOUR unique answers.

YOU CAN let go of exactly what limits YOU.

YOU CAN open up to new beliefs and possibilities that feel right for YOU.

YOU CAN welcome in the opportunities that are meant precisely FOR YOU and nobody else.

So, YOU CAN live to your highest potential & purpose.

That sounds awesome, but HOW CAN WE DO THIS…

It seems impossible!

Oh, that's only because nobody has taught you how to unlock the answers within yourself.

I guess not – so how do we do this?

Right, so in step 1, we want to find out what we are dealing with. We look at the symptoms we can spot at the surface level, which can guide us to the underlying problem. For example, a pattern is likely the symptom of something else.

A pattern?

Yes, a pattern is something we do repeatedly. Like a thought pattern (I can't do this or that) or a pattern of procrastination where you want to take action, but something, like an invisible force, is stopping you.

Our triggers and negative emotions are likely caused by something more significant than the situation itself.

In my work, I began seeing patterns that led me to identify the seven core truths and limiting beliefs. Most people had them and needed un-programming from them.

Ahhh, is this where the folders come from?

That's right. It is easier to address our issues if we can identify to which of these main seven categories our triggers, fears and patterns are connected to.

We also want to find out when and how they were created.

This detective work gets us to the root cause, and this is step one. Once we know what we are dealing with, we can let it go.

But how do we do this? You said these memories are all subconscious, and we can't remember them?

That's it – well remembered.

Do you also remember that every single one of our memories is still stored in our electromagnetic field?

Yes...

And do you remember that you are a vibrational being made of energy?

Yes, sort of...

So, every holographic memory also has a vibrational charge linked to it. If it is a happy memory, it will have a high vibration. If it is a challenging or scary situation, it will have a low, resistant charge connected to it. In addition, your core self will know the TRUTH about these memories. Because your core self is energy, and your memories are energy.

Wow, now let me get my head around this. Are you saying all my memories have an energy, and because my core self is also energy, it knows the truth? What is this truth you are talking about?

OK, so say the limiting belief that you are not good enough was created on Christmas Day when you were three years old. Your core self and energy remember this because it is stored as a holographic memory. It remembers WHO was there. It remembers WHAT was said, and it very clearly recalls that you were not happy that your older brother got this fantastic present and you only got something half the size. It remembers how unfair it felt to you. It remembers that you concluded this all happened because you were:

"NOT GOOD ENOUGH"

otherwise, you would have got exactly what you wanted. This can all be buried deep in your subconscious, even if your conscious brain does not recollect this event.

Yeah, right, even if that was the case - how could I get this information out of my subconscious?

You can do this by tapping into your inner guidance and energy.

How would I do that?

You can do so by "muscle testing", also known as truth or false testing.

Sorry? I do what?

OK, so imagine your body is made up of energy, and your memories are energy, and this energy knows if something is true or false for you. Then, you can get to the root cause by using your body as a tool.

My body as a tool?

Yes!

Are you mad?

OK, please, hear me out... You are so very near to understanding the power within you and how you can get to all your answers.

OK, go on... How do I use my body to get the answers?

You SWAY!

I WHAT!?!

You ask a YES or NO question and let your body talk by observing how it moves or "sways" like a pendulum.

Really, how does this work?

Your body can swing back and forth like a pendulum. Very simplified: If something is TRUE, your body tends to sway forward, and your body tends to sway backwards If something is false or untrue.

Hmmm... I am not convinced. How does this work?

The sway is an Ideomotor response. It bypasses your conscious awareness because it is a completely automatic reflex.

Really?

Yes, it's similar to the pupils in your eyes dilating or contracting to adapt to the light. They widen when it gets dark to let more light in and contract when it gets sunny to protect your eyes from the brightness. This is an automatic muscle response you don't consciously make.

So why does it go forward or backwards?

This is connected to what resonates with you and what doesn't.

I don't understand. Can you give me an example?

Imagine you are talking to two friends who tell you a story or a fact and explain it in great detail, but there is a big difference between them...

In scenario one, your friend shares something that interests you, and you are keen to hear ALL the details...

In scenario two, your friend tells you about something you have heard before you know you are NOT interested in because you find it boring.

How is this relevant?

It can explain what happens in the energy of our body.

How?

OK, tell me what happens to your body when you are interested and want to hear more. Would your body lean in and get closer to catch every word?

Yes, probably!

OK, and in scenario two, would your body do the same, get closer? Or would it lean backwards to distance itself from what it is not interested in?

Yes, I guess it would go back, but why does it happen?

It happens because of resonance and dissonance.

If something resonates with you and your energy says YES to it, you go forward. If something doesn't resonate with your energy, your body responds with a NO, and you go backwards. That's how the sway works.

So, if our sway goes forward, our body says YES?

If our sway goes backwards, our body says NO?

Correct. There are a few exceptions to why our sway can be confused and not give us straightforward answers, but as a rule, a forward sway is a YES, and a backward sway is a NO. This is how you can get to your answers in your subconscious.

So how do we SWAY, and how do we use it?

We sway by standing legs hip-width apart with a relaxed and grounded body. Then, we ask a yes or no question and wait for the body to respond.

Can I test it?

Yes, you can start testing your sway by asking questions you already know the answer is TRUE for you.

How to SWAY

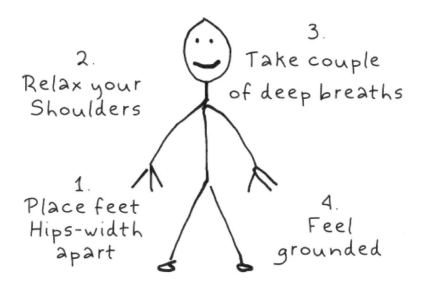

2.
Relax your
Shoulders

3.
Take couple
of deep breaths

1.
Place feet
Hips-width
apart

4.
Feel
grounded

5. Ask a YES or NO question

So, you could ask, for example:

Is my name (insert your name here)?

Was I born in (insert your birth month here)?

You should get a FORWARD sway for a YES.

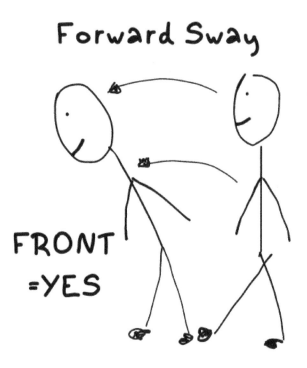

Then you can test with something you know is NOT true for you.

You could ask:

Is my name (insert a made-up name here)?

Was I born in (insert different month here)?

Now you should get a BACKWARD sway for a NO.

Backward Sway

BACK
=NO

Does it always work?

Sometimes, it can take a little time to get the hang of it. Your sway may be ever so slight until you get to know it. It can also be affected if you are dehydrated, on medications, over-tired or stressed.

(There are other ways to muscle test if someone cannot stand and sway. They could try a head sway, for example)

But rather than worrying, why don't you give it a go NOW and test if it works for you?

See this chair here?

CHAPTER 15
STEP ONE: FIND OUT

Yes…So what do I do?

Ask your body: "IS THIS A CHAIR?"

Really?!

Yes, go on…stand with your legs slightly apart, take a couple of nice deep breaths & relax your shoulders.

OK, what then?

You DO step one…and find out…

Now, look at this chair and ask yourself, "IS THIS A CHAIR?" Then feel into your body if you can feel a slight pull…

OK: "Is this a chair?"

WOW… I've moved forward!!!

That's it, Kiddo! That's your sway… Now try the other way!

Look at the chair and ask your body, "IS THIS A TABLE?"

OK; "Is this a table?"

And?

Not so much movement there, just a slight pull backwards.

That's OK…it takes some time to fine-tune your sway response. It should become more obvious the more you use and practise it…

Also, your sway will react stronger to some questions than to others.

Why is that?

It depends on how much energy is connected to the question.

If something is VERY true for you, it is likely that your forward sway will be stronger; also, if something doesn't resonate at all with you, your backward sway might be more pronounced. If you ask about something insignificant, your sway may be very slight.

So, I can ask my body questions and get an answer.

Can I ask it anything?

Yes, you can ask anything and get an answer based on what is true for you. However, the sway won't be able to give you answers outside of you, and it cannot predict the future. So, if you are thinking of using it to sway on the lottery numbers – I am afraid this won't work.

Aw, I was about to ask this...

But don't be too disappointed. The sway is still a very powerful tool that can help you to un-program yourself.

So, how do I use this to un-program myself from the stuff I don't want?

Great question!

So, we take the issue, the trigger, or the emotions and ask what it is connected to...Is it connected to a limiting belief? If yes, we can check each one.

Is the trigger connected to NOT FEELING SAFE?

Is this unwanted pattern connected to the belief that I AM NOT GOOD ENOUGH?

I see... the Sway tells me a YES or a NO. And what, then?

Then you can ask more clarifying questions about when this belief first started. Remember, we want to ask detective questions when, how, and why. This can bring us way back to the first event...

Why is this relevant?

Because the further back in time and the closest to the original event, the more we can un-program. Imagine the files that hold all your memories; they are stored in date order. The first memory is number one...and the next ones are added afterwards.

The further we can go back, the more memories of a similar kind we can let go in one go, making un-programming so much easier.

I am not sure I have completely grasped this concept yet, but go on.

So, I am trying to say that we don't need to let go of every memory individually. We can ask how often we have had a certain limiting belief. So, in your lifetime, you may have thought (consciously or subconsciously) 100 or 1000 times the thought:

"I am not good enough"

Over time, this became a belief. So, if you can get to the first time you thought, "I am not good enough," you can let go of the resistant energy of all those in one go.

NOW I get it! It's a bit like catching thoughts and memories like a ton of fish in a net and getting rid of them in one go.

Catching your limiting thoughts

Yes, I guess if you want to visualise your memories, thoughts and beliefs of a similar kind as FISH of a certain type and catch them all by going back to when they first started, then this is quite a good analysis. You can remove them from your subconscious and let them go by catching them this way,

So, I can set them free?

Yes, you can set them free as the energy they are - then they are no longer in your energy field...

This is Step TWO.

OK, let me recap. Step ONE is:

Doing the detective work to find out what we are dealing with by using the SWAY. We find out what triggers us. When it started, and how many limiting beliefs or thoughts are connected?

Yes, you could also describe them as resistances...

Resistances?

Yes, remember the invisible force that acts like a magnet – any negative thought or belief is a resistant thought that can hold you back like a magnet.

OK, so how can I let them GO?

Once you get to a "number" of how many you have, you ask if you can let them go.

How?

Well... you just ask: "Can I release them now?" And, if you get a YES, you can use the "LET GO statement" to let them go...

A LET GO Statement?

CHAPTER 16
STEP TWO: LET GO

Yes, you describe what you want to let go; you say it out loud three times and then check back in to see if they have gone.

Whaaat?? Are you kidding me? Like a spell or a silly chant? How would this work?

It works on the principle of energy and the power of your focus and intention.

I don't think I understand.

Do you remember I told you that your HEART is your body's most powerful energy centre? It creates the electromagnetic field around you, which stores all your memories.

Yes – I remember, but how would a brief statement let go of my programming?

Well, you see your throat and your voice connect directly to your heart. By focusing on WHAT you want to let go of with the power of your intention and commanding with the power of your voice, you can shift the energy that makes up those memories and release them out of your energy field.

Like the fish out of the net?

Yes, like the fish out of the net. Lol.

OK Great! Then please tell me about this LET GO Statement.

Sure thing… It is a statement repeated three times to clear as much as possible in one go.

So, here is an example of letting go of limiting beliefs about "not being good enough."

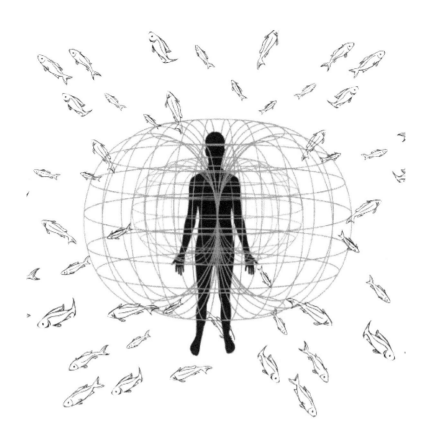

"I choose to LET GO of:

*the 500 limiting beliefs of "not being good enough"
that were first created when I was three years old.
I release them from my energy NOW: from all
TIME, SPACE, REALITY & LEVELS of
CONSCIOUSNESS. "*

Then, repeat a further two times.

And then what?

Then you check if they have GONE.

How?

By asking your body, using the sway again.

Ahh, like double-checking?

Yep, like double-checking...

What if they have not gone yet?

You can check how many remain and repeat the statement until they are gone.

Does this work every time?

Some beliefs are harder to find because they are hidden on different levels or have other things connected, then you need a few extra tricks up your sleeve, but this is the principle of how it works.

Can they come back after I let them go?

No, they don't come back – what's gone is gone, BUT remember the layers of the onion. You will come upon different layers of similar beliefs as you go through life, especially if you want to grow and create a better life for yourself.

How so?

For example, when you want a better-paid job that requires you to take more responsibility than in your current position and takes you out of your comfort zone. You may have to learn new skills, and if you get the job, you might not feel confident in the beginning. That's when you will probably hit new layers of your limiting beliefs. You doubt you can do it. You feel out of your depth; you fear they might find out that you don't have what it takes... It's different for all of us.

So, it's not done in one GO?

No, I wish, but you are meant to do this bit by bit. By removing the layers slowly, you begin to understand gradually who you are underneath. It's a process of transformation and takes time. Like it takes time for a caterpillar to turn into a butterfly, following the natural process gives you time to integrate so you can remember who you are, and this is your purpose.

I see... so, what are the other two steps, and why do we need them when we have already let go of our programming?

Ahhh...

Now, you see, letting go is only half of the process. What do you think happens when you let go of "the fishy files" from your limiting belief folders?

Well – I guess they are gone...

OK, and what happens when you delete files from a computer?

Hmmm. Not sure what you mean. They are gone, and there is empty space?

Exactly, you have freed up space in your energy field. So now comes the juicy part where you decide what you want instead.

What do you mean?

I mean, you want to un-program yourself for a reason, right?

If you feel lost, you want to find yourself.

If you feel confused, you want to find clarity.

If you've been procrastinating, you want to take action finally.

If you feel scared, you want to feel more confident.

If you feel unsure, you want to feel certain.

Ahh... I see it's going from the old way to a new way of being...

That's it, and you get to decide what that looks like!

CHAPTER 17

STEP THREE: OPEN UP

So, step THREE is about OPENING UP to new positive expectations. You decide how you want to feel and what you want to believe instead. In step three, you decide what is going to go into your

WELCOME IN statement, which you say out loud in step FOUR.

Oh, you mean like affirmations?

Yes, it's exactly like affirmations, but they will be much more powerful when you welcome them in because you have created the space in your energy field.

Does this mean I fill that space with something positive?

You are very smart!

Yes, you don't want to leave the space empty and get it accidentally filled with something not so positive. That's why the FOUR steps of F.L.O.W. should be done one after the other before going back to your everyday life.

OK, I've got you!

So, how do I get my positive affirmations?

You can write them down, or you can probably make them up when you get more practice. In the beginning, it could be helpful to look at what you've just LET GO of and then decide on the best things to welcome in to achieve your desired outcome.

If you felt stressed, welcome in more feelings of calm & tranquillity.

If you've just let go of limiting beliefs about "Not being good enough", you could welcome in "feeling confident in your abilities."

So, this means we are letting go of something negative and replacing it with a positive.

I like the sound of that, even if it seems a bit silly with this funny statement.

That's right...it's very simple, but don't underestimate how powerful these statements are. I will tell you more in a little while, but first, let's finish going through the four steps.

Let's re-cap:

Step 1: You FIND OUT what limits you by using the "detective sway".

Step 2: You LET GO what limits you by using the LET GO Statement, the power of your voice, focus & intention.

Step 3: You OPEN UP to new positive expectations by deciding what you want instead.

Step 4: You WELCOME IN using the positive affirmation statement, the power of your voice, focus & intention.

CHAPTER 18
STEP FOUR: WELCOME IN

Will it sound like a hocus pocus focus spell out of Harry Potter, lol?

Ahhh, well, you liked catching your limiting "fishy" beliefs in an imaginary net, and you have let them go from your electromagnetic field. You might as well do a bit of magic to bring in the good stuff. What do you say – are you on board for a bit of a bonkers journey?

I think I am already on it...

I guess you are – I am just checking to see if you want to hop off.

Nope, still on board, Captain, so let's go.

Let's do this step 4!

Righty Ho, let's go...

So, Step 4 is very similar to Step 2 in terms of statement. You welcome in the stuff you want instead of letting go of what you don't want. But there is a difference in how you stand.

How do I stand?

Yes, when you do step 4, you also have your legs hip-width apart, but now you take your arms up into the air to create a V-shape.

Why?

As you stand with your arms open, you create a funnel shape. When you say your affirmations, you are "calling in" what's wanted. Imagine it like a wish list to the universe. As you say them, you want to show the universe you are OPEN to receiving what you are asking for.

I see, OK, so tell me the statement.

Right, it can be something like this:

"I welcome in feeling confident in my abilities and trust that I am more than good enough.

I welcome this into my energy NOW

Into all TIME, SPACE, REALITY & LEVELS of CONSCIOUSNESS. "

"

Then, repeat twice more.

And that's it?

Yes, that's it. Of course, you can make it longer. You can pack as much good stuff in as you like... this is just a quick example to run you through the four steps of F.L.O.W.

OK, I "sort of" get the concept because I have heard of positive affirmations before, and it also makes sense to get rid of the old, unwanted stuff...

But can I ask you, HOW is this actually supposed to "work"? You said you would explain more...

PART IV
STEPPING INTO YOUR POWER

CHAPTER 19

UNDERSTANDING
THE LAW OF ATTRACTION

Kiddo, I must say, you DO surprise me...

When we started this conversation, I wasn't sure if you were open or ready for any of this. But look at YOU, fully engaged and eager to learn more.

I guess I was ready to do something about feeling so LOST - and then you appeared...

Do you know there is a famous saying:

"When the Student IS Ready, the Teacher WILL Appear"?

No, I didn't know that... and I am not sure I fully understand it.

OK, this is a great way to explain how ALL of this works...

Remember, I told you we are part of this universe and are not separate but fully connected.

Yes, I remember.

Now, this fantastic universe has what are called "Universal Laws" that keep things in balance and harmony. There are many different ones and one extremely powerful one...

Universal Laws? Like rules of what you can and cannot do and a court that judges over you?

Not quite like this...

The Universal Laws are more of an energy and invisible force that is always switched on. The best way to imagine them is if you think of them like "GRAVITY".

Gravity?

Yes, gravity is a force that keeps you firmly here on Earth without you floating off into the atmosphere. It is invisible, always at work and works for everyone – even if they are unaware. This is the nature of the Universal Laws that rule this universe.

I didn't know that…

That's the thing. Not many people know that these laws even exist – again, I don't think they are being taught in school yet.

So, here is the thing… if you want to understand how the world works and you want to thrive, it is really helpful to understand these laws.

How can they help me?

Understanding your power, the power of these laws, and how they interact gives you greater control over what you attract and manifest into your life. Knowing the rules means you can adjust your actions and behaviours to help you achieve what you want. It means you can consciously work with the universe rather than not knowing what's going on and why unwanted things are happening to you.

Wow… I am not sure what to say…I think I am speechless.

So, are you saying I can take control of my life by understanding these laws?

Yes, ABSOLUTELY, but it is a learning process like everything. First, you want to learn what they are, then recognise them when you see evidence in your everyday life. Then, you learn how to interact with them by adjusting your thoughts and actions.

OK – can you teach me, PLEEEAASE?

I love your enthusiasm, but it's pretty late, and you have already learned so much today. I don't want to over-stretch or overwhelm you. Besides, as much as I like chatting with you, there is somewhere I need to be shortly...

Oh, please, please, please, please, pleeeeeaaaase

Alright, I can see you are so keen and interested; believe me, there is SOOO much great stuff out there to learn. I couldn't possibly teach you all I know in the next half an hour...

Here is what I suggest. Before I go, I will teach you about the most powerful universal law and the basics. This gives you a great starting point. Together with the STEPS TO F.L.O.W., you can begin your un-programming and re-programming. What do you say?

That sounds SUPER – I am very grateful to you for sharing this with me.

OK then, let's dive in... Let's teach you about the powerful Law of Attraction.

Are you ready, my friend?

Extremely ready, so tell me about the Law of Attraction and why it is so powerful.

OK, so let me tell you what it is first. The Law of Attraction rules that we attract into our life (and our awareness) what we focus on and what is of the same energy and vibration as us.

This law is the most powerful because it interacts directly with us humans in every single moment, and like gravity, it is there whether we are aware of it or not.

So, HOW does it work?

Remember that I told you that your electromagnetic field has different purposes?

Yes...

Not only does it store your holographic memories, but it is also your powerful human Wi-Fi. It sends out signals and pulls things towards it because it is electro-MAGNETIC.

Do you mean like a giant MAGNET?

Yes, that's right, and it is always switched on 24/7, 365 days a year.

So, how does it send out the signals?

The signals are your thoughts, beliefs, and emotions, and are determined by what you focus on and what you give your attention to.

Remember I told you about your emotions and vibrations?

Yes, they can be high vibrations or low vibrations.

That's right... and that's the signal you are sending out. Every moment, you transmit a specific frequency signal into the universe. The better you feel, the more positive you are. If you are focused on what goes right, you send a high-vibration signal.

This is the unconscious signal you emit to the universe at every moment. The universe receives this signal like a message that says: "Can I please have more stuff like this!" And because you are sending the message, your magnetic energy field attracts and magnetises it into your life. If you feel good and are focused on the positive, you are more likely to attract the things you like and want more of...

But this is not what is happening to most people, right?

I can see a lot of unhappy people who are frustrated and worried.

Spot on. Most of us are NOT attracting what we want because we are sending out mixed signals. High and low signals fluctuate moment by moment. Some of us are signalling more consistent low signals and, as a result, struggle to get anywhere with our desires.

Like me? Is that why I felt lost?

Quite possibly, you see, if you feel down and uncertain, you tend to be at the bottom half of the emotional scale. That makes attracting, spotting the right opportunities or taking inspired action much harder.

So, you are saying the quality of the signal I am sending out is responsible for what I magnetise back into my life?

That's right

But HOW do I know what signal I am sending out?

Oh, that's easy... your emotions can tell you in every moment how you are doing!

My emotions?

Yes, you remember every emotion is a frequency? And your feelings can tell you if your "human thoughts" agree and align with your Seven Core Truths. If you don't feel good, there is a resistance between you and your core self.

Yes, I remember now. So, feeling good is the key?

You've GOT IT...

You can use your core self & your emotions to guide you moment by moment.

Guide me where?

Your emotions can guide you ANYWHERE you like.

They can guide you to your answers.

They can guide you to your onion layers and fishy beliefs, so you can let them go with the Steps to F.L.O.W.

They can guide you to find your authentic self.

They can guide you to step into your power.

They can guide you to live a life of your highest potential & purpose.

Your emotions are your compass and the key to unlocking the answers within yourself.

Wow, I said I didn't like my emotions and was fed up with them.

Yes, your emotions are the key to your power. They tell you if you are in alignment or not.

You mentioned the word "alignment" before, and I sort of get it. But can you explain it a bit more?

Of course

So, you understand that there are the two parts of you? Your CORE self that is connected to the universe and your human self that has forgotten? These two parts exist, even when your human self doesn't know about them.

They travel parallel paths if you like.

Like on a dual-carriageway?

Yes, if you like…

Imagine your core self has the Sat-Nav because it is connected to the universe. It has access to higher consciousness and has a good overview of how the world works. It knows where you are and where you want to go.

OHHHKAAAY…and then I guess you will tell me there is me, the human self, who doesn't know where I am going

Well, yes, you are right. That's why you are lost…You don't know you have YOUR core self by your side that can show you the easiest route.

So, what happens when we don't know the core self is there?

We are journeying through life, and we try this path and that path, and we can get a bit lost.

So, what's the answer?

The answer is awareness and alignment – we don't know what we don't know…. That's why so many people feel lost or hopeless. The first big step is becoming aware that we can influence what we attract into our lives. By becoming aware that there is another way of operating. By becoming aware of The Universal Laws and that our emotions are our guidance on how to come into alignment and harmony with our core self.

Once we know our inner guidance, we can start co-creating with the universe.

Co-creating with the Universe?

What do you mean?

Yes, life becomes easier when we understand that we are integral to everything around us. We are not separate; we are connected to everything because everything is energy. This table, this chair, you and I are all made of energy and are connected in this energy field. Our thoughts and beliefs are energy and determine what we attract into our lives. So, if we want to control what we attract, we can only do so by taking full responsibility for our thoughts and emotions.

Hang on; you are going too quickly...how do I take control?

You take control by co-creating with the universe...

How?

By becoming a vibrational match and aligned with what you want

Or as Abert Einstein famously quoted:

"Everything is energy and that's all there is to it. Match the frequency of the reality you want and you cannot help but get that reality. It can be no other way.

This is not philosophy.

This is physics."

CHAPTER 20

CO-CREATING WITH THE UNIVERSE

How can I take control & co-create with the universe?

To take back control of what happens in your life, you must take responsibility for EVERYTHING...

Why do I need to take responsibility for everything?

Taking responsibility means you take complete control of your "ability to respond". This means that whatever happens, you choose how you respond. If something unwanted happens, you have the power and the choice of how you respond. You can go and blame it on the circumstances or the people involved and become the victim of a situation. Or you can choose to take responsibility and see why this may have happened. Sometimes, when things don't work out the way, we hope it is because we have overlooked something or there is a lesson to be learned.

I don't know... this sounds like hard work. Why should I take responsibility for everything when someone else created something unwanted?

Sorry, I didn't mean you need to take responsibility or the blame for something that happens because of somebody else's doing. Taking responsibility is purely about what you choose to do with it.

What do I do with it?

Yes, even if you cannot influence what is happening around you, you still have the POWER on how you respond.

So, for example, something unwanted is happening. You can choose to blame the people or the situation responsible for it.

Yes, and if something or someone is clearly at fault, why wouldn't I blame them?

Well, you can go down the blame route. This is your free choice. But notice how this makes you feel. If you blame something outside for an unwanted situation, you have no power over it. Then, it has power over you and how you feel. You become the victim of the situation or circumstances.

What? I don't believe this...

You don't believe this? Shall I give you an example?

Yes, please.

So, imagine you are supposed to meet with a good old friend (who you know tends to be late), and you are meant to go to this great show in town. You arranged to meet outside the theatre, and your friend does not arrive at the agreed time. The theatre doors close, and still no sign of your friend. What do you think? What do you feel?

I feel angry and annoyed.

Why do you feel angry and annoyed?

Because my friend is late and spoiled the evening by not showing up on time....

You might be in the right to blame your friend because of the circumstances, BUT can you see how the blame creates negative emotions inside of you? By blaming your friend, you become the victim of the situation. You are at the effect of the situation and have no power over how you feel. This means you have given your power away...

I don't see what I could do differently or why I should.

Ahhh, you see, blaming is a knee-jerk reaction we do if we are unaware of what is happening in our energy. So, while it may be justified to blame, it creates negative emotions. And when we understand that negative emotions mess up our high vibe signal, then it becomes something we may want to pay attention to.

Because our signal is responsible for what we attract into our life?

That's right. While it may be justified to feel angry, your anger will create a low-energy vibration and affect the signal you send into the universe. This, then, will affect what happens next. So, in the example of meeting your friend, the evening will most likely take a sour turn if you are angry and annoyed.

So, what are the alternatives?

An alternative approach would be to see the situation as neutral. Your friend is late, and there is nothing you can do about that. The theatre doors are closed, and you missed the start of the show. How you respond to this will determine what happens next. As we said in scenario one, you can get angry and annoyed, which will probably mean a tension-filled evening.

The alternative is to see this as an opportunity to learn something and make the best of it. So, you could take away from the experience that whenever you meet this friend again, you will meet extra early to avoid this kind of thing happening again (=lesson learned).

You can also see that missing the show created the opportunity to catch up and chat with your friend more than if you had sat in a show for three hours (= positive outcome).

Well, this sounds like viewing life through rose-tinted spectacles.

OK, I agree it does, but the important thing is HOW you want to feel at the end of the day. Do you want to feel good and take back control of your power, or do you want to feel angry and frustrated and give your power away?

Well, if you put it like this. Of course, I want to feel good and take back control of my power.

But how does this help me practically?

OK, so it helps you in two ways.

First, if you can shift your thoughts and see the opportunities rather than the downside in any given situation, you create better-feeling emotions. So, your number one win is that you FEEL BETTER.

Secondly, when you feel better, you send a higher vibration signal....

And when I send a better signal, I attract better things into my life?

That's it!

This is how you co-create with the universe. The more deliberate you send out better signals, the more you will manifest your desires. It takes practice and awareness, but once you know you have a choice (in every moment) how you respond, you can take back control.

So, what does this look like on a practical level?

How do I start taking back control?

How do I start manifesting my desires?

The power is in the NOW...

The power is in the NOW – what's that supposed to mean?

OK, the power of NOW is a profound yet very simple concept and the TRUTH...

Man... what now? I feel this will be going straight over my head....

OK, let me say this in the simplest way possible. The opportunity to create your dream life and fulfil your desires is only possible NOW. This very moment you are in right now. Because there is NO past and NO future where you can create in. When you get to tomorrow, you will be again in a NOW moment, not in the future. You can think of what your future may look like, but to get there and achieve what you want can ONLY be done in the NOW. Every moment, you can choose how you think, feel, react, and how you take action. Your thoughts, emotions, and actions in the now will be responsible for your future results. Does this make sense?

Sort of. Are you saying whatever happens in the future depends on my thoughts and actions in the NOW?

What about what happened in the past? Does this not affect me now or in the future?

That's a brilliant question... especially since I explained that we have all been programmed. The answer is YES & NO.

YES, your past and your programming will affect you if you are unaware of it, and limiting beliefs are running your conscious and subconscious thoughts and emotions and affect the actions you take or don't take.

And the answer is NO because they don't have to affect you when you can let go of that old, unwanted programming. And guess what? In every moment, your emotions tell you if you are on track or not.

If you feel negative emotions, they will let you know of a limiting belief or a bit of conditioning, and then you can choose how you respond in the NOW. To let them go or keep them.

Why would I want to keep them?

Many people hold on to their limiting beliefs because this is who they think they are. They are not aware that they even have a choice. YOU know NOW that you have a choice, and

I am glad you want to shift what is no longer serving you and what limits you.

So, what happens when I start doing what you say?

I assume you become increasingly aware of what is going on in your experience. You will notice more how you feel. You will become more aware of the thoughts that are going through your mind. You will become attuned to how your reaction to things will create different outcomes. You will notice when things go well and when things could have worked out better. Life will give you more opportunities to practise those.

This is also part of your purpose...

It is to figure out how your interactions will create more desired outcomes. You will learn about yourself. Every time you hit a limiting belief or a layer of programming, you are given the opportunity to heal that limiting story of yours. You can get to know your authentic self. Discover your values and passion, and get to know your desires. This is all part of your purpose for being here. While your core self may be the same, your avatar is new in this lifetime. So, your purpose is to learn what it likes and dislikes. What brings it joy and what it doesn't like...

So, it's my purpose to find out what brings me joy?

Yes, that's your purpose – if you don't achieve anything else but can find what brings you joy and happiness, then you have lived a purposeful life.

But that's not it, surely?

There is always more. You live in a universe of endless opportunities and possibilities. The fun starts properly when you realise you are co-creating with the universe. Every action and thought of yours has a ripple effect. As you become more attuned and aligned with what feels good, things become easier. You will know when you are in alignment and F.L.O.W. because synchronicities will happen. You will meet the right people at the right time. Opportunities will open up for you.

That's when life becomes FUN.

So, you are saying the only power I have is in the NOW, and if I change how I think, feel and take action, things will change for the better? And my emotions tell me whether I am on track or not.

Oh, I am impressed! I couldn't have said it better myself. That's the journey. This is how you co-create with the universe: one moment, one thought, one emotion, one action at a time.

This is how you can create the magical, abundant, joyful, happy and fulfilled life you are meant to experience!

Wow!

I guess…

I better start paying attention to my thoughts and my emotions then…

CHAPTER 21

UNDERSTANDING YOUR POWER

That's great. Becoming aware of your thoughts and emotions is the key to getting started. This fine-tunes you and connects you to all your senses, including your sixth sense.

My sixth sense? What do you mean?

Yes, your sixth sense is your intuitive power. We all have intuitive powers within us, even if we don't know it, because we are not fine-tuned to them yet!

How does it work?

Well, your SWAY is part of your intuitive power because it taps into the energy of your electromagnetic field. Your energy field has another purpose apart from storing your holographic memories. It also reads the energy of your environment.

It reads the energy of the environment. How?

OK, let me ask you a question. Have you ever walked into a room of people without hearing what was said, BUT you could sense the mood in the room?

Yes, that happens all the time. You just know if people are happy and relaxed or on edge! Are you saying my electromagnetic field is doing that?

Yes, that's right- because your electromagnetic field extends around you and literally enters the room before your physical body. Your energy field interacts with the energy field of the people around you, and it "reads" the energy. It can detect their mood by reading the frequency of their active vibration. This is how we can pick up on other people's moods. How we receive this information can vary from person to person depending on our clairs.

Our clairs? What on earth is that?

Your clairs are your different intuitive senses through which you receive the information. The four most known intuitive senses are:

Claircognizance is an "inner knowing".

Clairvoyance is when you can "see an image" in your mind's eye.

Clairaudience, you might hear an inner voice telling you something.

Clairsentience is when you feel the emotions of others in your own body.

Ah, like an empath?

Yes, that's right! A lot of empathic people can pick up on the feelings of others.

OK, but how does this help me?

Your intuitive gifts are your superpowers and your inner guidance. They can help you in the decision-making process to assess what is right for YOU. Remember, you have all the answers within yourself. What is right and best for you does not necessarily need to be true for somebody else. You are unique; you are here for a specific reason and purpose, and you can only discover what that is if you listen within.

I don't hear much... I don't think I have those intuitive gifts!

Of course, you have! They are just buried underneath the layers. That's why you want to remove those. Bit by bit, you chip away until the real YOU becomes visible.

The REAL ME?

Yes, your AUTHENTIC SELF

My AUTHENTIC SELF?

Yes, you are AUTHENTIC when your core self and avatar are in harmony. In alignment and flow, knowing you are significant.

That's your PURPOSE, too, to strip back the layers, discover the real you, and then step into your power by nurturing your intuitive gifts and talents.

Why?

Because when you are your authentic self and embrace your power, you are getting closer and closer to living your highest potential and purpose.

What is this highest purpose?

Ahh... That's your purpose to discover...

While the journey to discover yourself is part of your purpose, your HIGHEST PURPOSE is something much bigger. It can be something that you've learned. Something you have overcome. Something you can teach. Something you can be an example of. Something that inspires others.

Something that leaves this world or the people in it in a better place. Something that makes a difference. Something that has a positive impact. Something that creates a shift or has a positive ripple effect. Something you would do even if there was no financial reward. Your highest purpose is a calling. Something you know at your core level that you are here to do.

Wow... that sounds deep- I have no idea what that could be...

Don't worry. I, too, had no idea but, trust me, you can get there. The path will unfold. You will discover what lights you up, what makes your heart sing. You will meet people on your way who will guide you. You will receive all the information you need.

The teachers will appear. Just follow the breadcrumbs. Follow your heart and intuition, and use your sway to help you.

Is that what you did?

Yes, that's right, when I felt lost (and down), there was this moment when I knew something had to change. I didn't know what and how, but I decided to look for answers. I felt disempowered and alone and didn't know where to turn to.

So, what did you do?

I listened to inspirational speakers and remember one of them saying:

"Happiness comes when you do the things that light you up... the things you would do for free, the something that is your purpose...!"

That really resonated with me.

So, you learned from that person?

No, that was just a seed planted.

It made sense that by finding my purpose and doing what I would love, I would feel more fulfilled and happier. But I didn't learn it from that person! He knew it was something inside of us that needed discovering, BUT he didn't have the answer to what my purpose would be for me.

So, what did you do?

Oh, I'll tell you what I did... I GOOGLED it.

You GOOGLED IT?!?

Yes, back then, I thought I could Google the answer and remember typing "how to find your purpose..."

And?

Surprise, surprise, I did NOT find the answer...But it started something...

What did it start?

It started me asking questions about myself, and it started me on my journey of personal growth and learning.

Just like you started today, right here, right now...asking me all your questions.

I see - so how did you get to where you are now? Have you found your purpose?

I got to where I am now, step by step. I listened to many inspirational speakers, life coaches & teachers. I learned about Mindfulness, NLP, Hypnosis, and The Universal Laws. I learned about the dynamics of life and happiness. Some things resonated, others didn't, but I kept following the trail that opened up for me. I followed what resonated and left other things aside – this is the key to finding your purpose. What resonates will bring you closer to finding your highest purpose. On the path of personal growth, you will learn and "up-level" bit by bit.

Can we not just find the best teacher and learn it all?

Ah, Kiddo, teachers and lessons come in many forms. It can be a friend telling you something that clicks something else into place. It can be something random you see on television that suddenly makes sense of something you've heard from a teacher or a technique many moons ago. Learning and expansion happen gradually over time.

Why is that?

It's because you are only ready for certain things. Your awareness and capacity to take on new concepts need to increase. Like your body when it was growing from a child into an adult. It would be too much of a shock to grow too quickly.

And only when you are ready, have the capacity and are curious enough will you find the answers to your questions like: Who are you? And why are you here?

Doesn't everyone want to know who they are and why they are here? Doesn't everyone want to know why they feel lost and want to do something about it?

Oh, you would be surprised. I thought that, too. But just because you and I are eager to discover answers, not everyone else is...

You see, the questions you asked and the answers you received today may not resonate with everybody. Some people who started reading this book will never get to this chapter because it doesn't resonate with them or not yet.

What do you mean by "Not Yet"?

Sometimes, we get presented with concepts and ideas that are too advanced. And we need to expand and grow, and then later on, they suddenly resonate, and that's OK...

Our life is like a puzzle.

The answers are the puzzle pieces. For a bit of information to make sense, we often need to connect other puzzle pieces first. That very piece of the puzzle only makes sense in connection with another.

So, only by bringing the different answers or puzzle pieces together will the bigger picture emerge.

And what is the bigger picture?

The bigger picture is YOU... Who you are deep down...who you are authentic, what your passion is and what your highest purpose might be.

Oh, is it really?

Yes, Kiddo, it's your purpose to puzzle the pieces together and let go of the bits that don't belong to your puzzle.

Do you mean the layers and the conditioning?

That's right, we all take things on board that are clogging us up and bury us underneath, and then we don't know who we truly are.

And we feel lost...

That's right... You can also feel low and heavy if you carry all the layers, resistant, energetic memories and beliefs around with you. It's like having a heavy bag on your shoulders.

But you have the power to change that.

How?

How? By having a greater awareness of all we have talked about here today...

You know you have your intuition and your guidance. You have the sway that tells you what resonates at a core level. You can uncover your limiting beliefs. You have a technique to let them go. You can align yourself to new possibilities. You have your emotions that guide you on the right path. And you will come across teachers and opportunities that will guide you back to your authentic self. And once you return to your authentic self, anything is possible.

CHAPTER 21

DISCOVERING YOUR AUTHENTIC SELF

I still struggle to understand what you mean when you say becoming my authentic self.

Am I not my authentic self right now?

Of course, deep down, you are your authentic self, but the layers of your beliefs shape how you behave.

We all take on roles and play those roles to fit in because we have learned what is expected of us in these roles.

Can you give me an example?

Of course, that's easy… everything that labels us makes us take on a role… when you were in school, you took on the label of a pupil. You learned how to behave to fit in. Being a child made you take on that role. Our mothers and fathers took on the roles of parents. At work, we took on the role of the employee. These roles come with an unspoken set of rules of what is expected, acceptable and what is not…

I see, so are you saying these roles are bad for us?

They are not necessarily bad for us if we can be authentic and express our individuality.

The problem is that these things are often in conflict, and we suppress our true nature to fit in. Or we don't even have a clue who we are without those roles. We take them on as our true identity.

The more roles we take on, the more we potentially lose our authentic selves.

Why is that?

Oh, it happens so gradually that most of us don't even question it... It's just how the world works. In life, we belong to a category of roles and play a part in each. We learn how to fit in; before we know it, we are like chameleons. We learn what behaviours get us the best results. So, we present ourselves in ways others approve of us and may even go out of our way to please people.

Surely that's not such a bad thing to please other people?

No, of course, there is nothing wrong with being nice to others, but if you are playing a role and pretending you like something when you don't, then you are not true to yourself. People pleasing can be unhealthy if you neglect your own needs and prioritise everyone else.

How is that?

Neglecting your wants and desires means you are potentially adding conditional layers. Whenever you put other people's needs before yours, you possibly say NO to yourself. You may deny your significance, and your core self can disappear under the layers until...

Until we feel LOST?

That's it, Kiddo, and then it can show up as anger or frustration, depression, anxiety, worry or fear because your core self wants to be honoured and heard. It wants YOU to shine and step into your power and highest potential. It wants you to get up to the top of that pyramid. It wants YOU to feel significant, powerful, abundant and FREE!

So, what's the answer...

The answer is doing the work! Doing what's necessary to let go of your programming and step into becoming your most authentic self.

That sounds quite selfish...

Yes, it is, and it must be...

Why?

Because you are the most important person in your life!

You came here to discover who you are, and so has everyone else. But only YOU can find out who YOU are and what your highest purpose is.

Hmmm...right, but I still wouldn't have a clue how to do this, and it is easy for you to say.

You seem to have done it! How did you get there?

Yes, Kiddo, I am in a good place now, but this work is never done. There is always another higher level you can aim for because there is always room for more growth and expansion.

So, how did you do it...

OK, there are four key things that I have discovered that can help you succeed on this journey:

1. Celebration of the positive & Commitment to letting go of the unwanted.
2. Curiosity & Consistency in doing the work.
3. Community & Connection – like-minded people to share the journey with.
4. Clarity & Confidence in the best approach and support to guide you.

Oh, just those four things...

How would I start?

You make it all sound so easy-peasy lemon squeezy.

I know, but trust me, things will fall into place when you are ready and want to do this. It's The Law of Attraction at work. If you have a desire for something and you don't resist it, then the teacher will appear. You will meet the right people and find the right approach for you. Sometimes, you try something, and it doesn't feel quite right. Then, you learn which approach NOT to take. We call this a clarifying experience.

A clarifying experience?

Yes, when you know what you don't want, you know better what you DO want. It gives you clarity.

So, if you say negative experiences are clarifying... are you saying, they are positive?

Yes, this is how you can flip a negative into a positive. You see, there is always a silver lining to everything. But most people are not taught how to flip things - instead, they are so focused on their problems and what goes wrong. This brings me to the first key point - celebration of the positive.

Oh yes, please tell me more about the four KEYS.

PART IV

THE JOURNEY & KEYS TO SUCCESS

CHAPTER 23

THE JOURNEY TO YOUR HIGHEST PURPOSE

Right, so do you understand that being on the journey IS the journey and is your purpose?

Well, sort of, but honestly, it just sounds like an excuse that you haven't reached the destination yet.

I know, Kiddo, but that is life… we can never get to tomorrow… because when tomorrow comes, it will be today, and another tomorrow will be ahead of you.

Oh, heck, that's a bit deep…

Yes, but it is the truth. It's what we talked about earlier and the power of NOW. It will make your journey easier if you understand that the aim is not to get to a specific point in your journey. That's why so many people are unhappy. They have this idea that they will be happy once they get to a certain point in their life. If only they can achieve this. Get that job, have that money, have that relationship, THEN they will be fulfilled. But that is not the case… They are chasing something only when they get there - there will be something else they need or want to achieve.

Are you saying that having goals and dreams is something bad?

No, I am not saying that at all… If you are happy in yourself and want to achieve more because it is fun. Because it is part of your growth journey, it's a great thing! I am talking about the many people chasing dreams because they are unhappy where they are. Their desire to achieve these things is not driven by fun and excitement but by lack, fear and worry.

If someone is focused on making more money and fearful that they might run out of money, then their real focus is on not having enough and is driven by a sense of lack rather than abundance. It will make their life harder to achieve this.

On the other hand, if you feel already abundant and are having fun testing out new ventures, you collaborate, and you enjoy experimenting, then opportunities to make more money will come easily because you already feel abundant.

So, are we back to the point that feeling good and having fun is the key to being on the right track?

Yes, I guess we are. You see, LIFE is not so difficult when you know the rules and keys to feeling good.

So, you mentioned that the journey is the journey...

Yes, enjoy the NOW, and by all means, know where you want to go, but be light-hearted about it. The more you can relax, the more enjoyable the ride will be. The journey should be one of ease and F.L.O.W. – that's when the right breadcrumbs will appear.

The breadcrumbs?

Yes, like stepping stones, showing you the next steps to take. The more you can come into alignment and flow, the easier it will get along the way.

But it takes some time to get there, right? What about all the layers of conditioning and programming?

Yes, they are there, but they don't need to frighten you. You can deal with them when you bump up against one. With the right approach & support, these resistant layers can be dissolved quickly.

So, are you saying there won't be any hard times ahead?

This completely depends on you.

We can all experience challenging or hard times. This is part of the human experience. How hard you will find them, how well you can cope and how quickly you can bounce back depends on how much baggage you carry around with you. Now that you know what negative emotions mean and have a technique to let go of your limiting beliefs, you can choose how long you are willing to endure discomfort or move on and feel better.

Hmmm, this sounds a bit too good to be true. How can I know that you are telling the truth?

Well, look out there... I agree. Some people suffer and have a terrible time. But likewise, so many people are thriving and having amazing lives. What do you think is the difference?

I don't know – LUCK, maybe?

No, it's not luck, although it might seem so to someone observing from the outside. But it has nothing to do with LUCK but all with how aligned and in F.L.O.W. they are with their desires AND how high their frequency and vibrational signal is.

So, are you saying it is all connected?

The better we feel, the better things we attract. And the more we are our authentic selves, the better we feel.

Yes, that's it. And don't worry... nobody is happy all the time. We all experience ups and downs. We all have negative or clarifying experiences. What counts is what you do when that happens. How you respond will affect how quickly you can bounce back to feeling good.

Do you mean the more aligned I become, the shorter the times I feel negative emotions?

That's right, over time, your emotional setpoint will go up. The more time you spend feeling good, the easier it is to recover from something unwanted because your batteries are charged. A little incident will not wipe you out when your batteries are full. It's merely a little dip in energy. But when you feel down and worried, and your batteries are already depleted, and something else happens, it can wipe you out completely.

So, feeling good keeps my batteries charged?

Yes, your happy juices keep them charged, and you thrive.

Is it really that easy?

Remember the seven core truths I mentioned right at the beginning?

Yes, sort of...

You want to keep them high on your priority list because this is what you want to align to.

What do you mean I want to align to them?

Your core self knows you are 100% safe, worthy, deserving & good enough. It completely believes you are loved, connected, unique, magnificent and significant.

You want to ensure that the human part of YOU also believes this. That's what we call alignment when your avatar and core self agree.

Why is this important?

Only when you have that foundation will you feel safe and confident to step into your power. Only then will you manifest abundance, feel completely free and at ease and create the life you want.

How can I start believing that this is all true about me?

That's the work, Kiddo!

You want to find & let go of your limiting beliefs. When you do this, you will get closer and closer to being 100% aligned to believing that you are safe, loved, connected, worthy, significant, powerful, abundant & free.

Ah, NOW I get it!

This is why we want to find the fishy limiting beliefs so we can free ourselves from them?

Yes, you free yourself from the beliefs, the programming and conditioning bit by bit, and eventually, what appears is the true YOU: "Your authentic self."

That makes sense and I like the sound of that.

So, would you like to learn about the Four Keys?

Yes, please!

160

CHAPTER 24

KEY ONE:
CELEBRATION & COMMITMENT

So, what do you mean by celebration & commitment?

OK, they are two things that are separate but go hand in hand.

By celebration, I mean celebrating what already goes well in your life and is the KEY to feeling good in the here and NOW.

You have the choice in every moment to find something to appreciate. There is always something to be grateful for, even if it's just that you have clean drinking water and are lucky enough to have woken up in the morning.

The more you focus on what goes well and celebrate even the smallest achievements and wins, the better you will feel. Focus on the positive, not the negative, and shift your focus whenever possible.

Yes, you said that before – yet so many people find so many things to complain about...

Yes, and that's what makes a HUGE difference to the signal you are putting out. The trouble is that many people are unaware they are messing up their signal by complaining, blaming, and moaning. Unfortunately, their habit is to focus on the negative and discuss it in depth. You can imagine this takes quite some effort to shift deliberately.

So, how can this be done?

Through the other key: Commitment!

Commitment?

Yes, until we are aware of what we are doing, i.e., messing up our signal by being focused on the negative, there is nothing we can do. But once we know we have a choice, we can take control of our emotions and the signal if we are committed.

Committed to deliberately focusing on what feels better. Committed to finding things to appreciate. Committed to NOT engaging in blaming circumstances or other people. Committed to using the tools and techniques that can shift the old programming. Committed to honouring your needs. Committed to prioritising yourself. Commitment to making the changes necessary to achieve your desires.

This sounds like a lot to commit to...

It may sound a lot, but remember, you just focus on one moment. In this little moment, you just choose how you want to respond. Suppose your friend comes up to you and wants to talk about something that went wrong or an unpleasant situation.

You have a choice in how you respond. You can choose to chime in and recall a situation where something similarly bad happened to you, OR you can decide not to engage in this way.

You have a choice when faced with a "negative scenario". You can choose to engage, which would put fuel on the fire and make it worse, OR you can put water on the fire and dampen it down.

Aha, you mean we just change how we respond?

Yes, you cannot totally avoid being exposed to people and circumstances that carry low-frequency energy, but you have the choice of what you do with it.

If you are committed to feeling good and sending out the best signal, then it just becomes a "game of choice", moment by moment.

And don't worry if you slip... You will get plenty more moments to get it right.

OK, that doesn't sound SO daunting when you put it like this. Each moment is another opportunity to improve.

That's right! Life will give you opportunities to improve all the time. This is part of our learning. Yet, most people see obstacles as something bad.

When you can see challenging situations as opportunities to grow and get to know yourself, then you have won half the battle.

Challenging situations are only challenging because we have not yet learned how to handle them. They bring us to our limits. When we give up and shy away, they will limit us in what we can achieve.

Remember, most of the time, it's only one of your own limiting beliefs that is kicking in. It's nothing to be afraid of because it cannot hurt you if you address it. It only hurts you by pushing it down, and that ultimately makes you unhappy.

Why is that?

Because your core self wants to grow and expand but is held back by the scared version of yourself (your "inner child") that felt out of his/her depth between the ages of 0 and 7.

This makes so much sense – we are unhappy because we are not living up to our potential because we are scared. So, then we are scared AND unhappy…

Yes, and if this goes on and on and on, you risk spiralling down until you feel lost and don't even know how you got there because it happened so gradually.

Yes, that sounds familiar…. OK, I think I can get more focused on what is going well in my life and celebrate this by appreciating what I already have.

What about commitment? Do you think you can commit to choosing thoughts that feel better? Are you committed to letting go of blaming other people or situations? Are you willing to commit to taking responsibility for your emotions?

This is trickier because I still believe that sometimes other things, people or circumstances ARE to blame!

Yes, that's a tricky one, especially if we are used to holding something or someone else responsible for what has happened. BUT and that really is a BIG, BUT you have the choice of how you react. They might be responsible for the outcome of a situation, but what goes on in YOUR emotions is 100% on YOU!

Remember, when you give these people or situations the power to dictate how you feel, then you give away your power.

I don't want to give my power away...

You can stay in your power if you take complete ownership of your emotions. If you are committed to taking full responsibility for how you feel, not only do you take back your power, but you also free yourself.

What do you mean?

I mean, once you get the hang of this, then you will become lighter and feel more inner freedom because you will feel less or unaffected by things that would have triggered you before.

Can you give me some examples?

Yes, negative comments – will not affect you because you understand that somebody's rudeness has nothing to do with you. It's their limited way of communicating. Instead of feeling offended, you can actually feel compassion for them.

When somebody lets you down, you don't take it personally any more. You are relaxed because you know these things can happen. Instead of being hurt and angry, you can give them the benefit of the doubt.

When someone cuts you up in traffic you eventually laugh and get on with your life.

I don't know how easy that will be... I can see that this would trigger me.

It's OK, Kiddo.

That's the journey. You will catch yourself getting triggered as you become more aware, and every time, you can hopefully catch it a little earlier. You will find more ways to release your thoughts and shift your focus so you get less triggered.

But how do I do this?

The easiest way, I find, is by deliberately looking at a triggering situation and asking myself: How can I think about this differently? Are there any (unknown) reasons why this person may behave like this? Maybe they felt triggered? Are they limited in their thinking? Can I let them off the hook for this?

OK, I see. I decide if it's worth getting hung up about it or not.

Yes, that's it...

But what if something really triggers me, and things escalate because I can't keep it together?

Then, you most likely hit a layer. If you cannot change your focus or reason about it, then it's probably a limiting belief that is triggered.

Then what do I do?

You can check with the sway... Do you want to give me an example?

Yes, for example, my colleague at work always leaves jobs lying around and expects somebody else to do the work

for them… and I am being triggered because it happens all the time. It annoys me, but I can't lose it because it might jeopardise things at work.

OK, I get it… so you think you feel triggered and annoyed because of your colleague's laziness?

Yes, that's right…

Ahh, you see, "the laziness" is just your "trigger", but there is more to it…

What do you mean more to it?

You need to look at what's underneath. Discover the real reason YOU feel annoyed, take full responsibility for how you feel, and don't give your power to other people. Because right now, if you are annoyed about the laziness of your colleague, he or she "controls" how you feel.

So, what's the real reason?

The real reason is within you. You might actually feel taken advantage of right now. A good chance is that this has happened before in other situations. Maybe you were always the most responsible of your siblings when you were younger. You were always the tidy one, and it even annoyed you back then that your siblings were lazy. But you did more anyway because you either wanted to or were expected to.

Maybe you felt that if you pleased others by doing more, you would be more liked and accepted.

Hmmm… you may have a point.

So, you see, the pattern on the surface is the LAZINESS of another person. Underneath is the belief "I am being taken advantage of", and underneath this is possibly the limiting belief. "I am not good enough & I am not loved and accepted" if I don't do…. XYZ.

Crickey, that's deep…

Yes, it is, but can you see that it also is quite simple… what triggers you is probably only a limiting belief that contradicts one of the Seven Core Truths. Then, you can get straight to the point.

So, what would I do then?

You could sway on it. Identify which limiting belief you are dealing with. When it was first created, and who was involved.

And then?

You LET IT GO & release it with the statement.

Ok, I think I can do that!

CHAPTER 25

KEY TWO:
CURIOSITY & CONSISTENCY

So, what about curiosity and consistency?

Yes, these are also key ingredients to feeling better and moving toward your highest purpose.

OK, please explain what you mean by curiosity and consistency.

Curiosity is probably the key ingredient to improving your life.

Let's face it: the reason why so many people are not on the journey to their highest purpose or even to living a fulfilled life is because they are NOT curious. They don't even question their existence or their circumstances. The trouble is that many people are programmed not to ask questions. Not to rock the boat. Whatever the reason, without curiosity or the willingness to ask questions, you will not start on the journey of personal growth.

Positive improvements only happen with change, the quality of the questions we ask, and the answers we receive.

Look at all the inventions in history. Things were invented to solve problems by people who asked questions. They all knew there had to be a solution; there had to be an answer that nobody else had thought of before. These genius people knew there had to be another way, and they kept asking different questions until they found an answer that solved the problem.

So, are you saying that we are the problem and we need to ask questions about ourselves?

I wouldn't call ourselves a problem. A puzzle may be a better way of describing it! We want to find an answer to who we really are. We want to discover what our values and desires are. Because only when you truly know yourself can you go in the direction of what you want. Without it, you just go around in circles and potentially feel lost.

So, people feel lost because they are not curious and they are not asking questions?

Yes, or they are not asking the RIGHT questions.

Not the right questions?

Yes, remember earlier I mentioned disempowering questions that keep you stuck because they are focused on the problem.

So, if you want to feel better and find solutions and answers, you need to be curious and ask empowering or liberating questions.

But aren't we focused on the problem when we ask about our limiting beliefs?

Good question! Yes, we are focusing on the problem, but with the intention of releasing the issue at root cause level. This way, we remove the trigger, like removing a thorn that is bothering you. And remember, once we let it go, we will focus on how we want to feel instead.

Like when we get to the limiting belief that we are "not good enough" because we feel taken advantage of for doing the extra work...

That's right; by letting this go, you will feel less triggered by your colleague because you no longer take it personally. If they are lazy, that doesn't mean they want to take advantage of you. Can you see how the trigger goes away by removing the root cause?

So, curiosity and asking the right questions about yourself will guide you, and then you just need to be consistent at doing this...

Like going to the gym?

Yes, that's right, to see results, it takes consistency, like building muscles... You won't see results straight away, but like with commitment, consistency will, over time, create the results you want.

What can I expect if I do this work?

I would think that your outlook on life will be more positive. You will feel more joyful and happy in yourself, and that will have a positive impact on your relationship with others.

You will feel less stressed and more relaxed and at ease. You will have more energy because your batteries are being recharged.

You will have more focus and clarity. As a result, your work will flow better, and you can achieve your goals more easily.

This all sounds good and worth the effort...

Absolutely! So, do you think you feel curious and are up for doing consistent work?

Oh, I am definitely curious. I have wanted to find a solution for such a long time. I wanted to understand myself and why I am the way I am. And I am curious to find the answer within myself. I think if I can get to know who I really am, then things will get better. I will feel more positive and get a better idea of what I want to do with my life. I know there must be more… I can feel there is a reason for being here, and I am curious about what that is.

That's great, Kiddo… it seems we were meant to meet and have this conversation.

Do you know what…

What?

I always had a strange feeling there would be a way to find the answers. I always knew I could somehow find out how the world works. Why we are here and what our purpose is.

Of course, you did – and do you know why that is?

Why?

It's because YOUR CORE self was guiding you…. That's your intuition talking. Your inner knowing or your gut instinct.

So, it is there…

Yes, it was there all along... I was right; you were not as LOST as you thought. Now, all you need is consistently chipping away at the layers, and you will get to your authentic self. And then anything is possible...

Wow, I suddenly feel really optimistic.

I thought it was really hard work, and I had no clue what the solution would be.

And if I am honest, I still don't know HOW I get started.

But is this really true?

What do you mean?

Well – you have learned...

1. that you have all the answers within yourself

2. about the seven CORE TRUTHS and the contradicting limiting beliefs

3. the four steps to F.L.O.W. to shift things

4. and now you are learning about the 4 KEYS that will help you align to those core truths.

Yes, I know, but I still feel unsure what to do with it...

OK, that's because you have not heard about the two remaining KEY elements: Community & Connection and Clarity & Confidence.

CHAPTER 26

KEY THREE:
COMMUNITY & CONNECTION

OK, so tell me about community and connection.

Of course, this one is dear to my heart because when I felt lost, a big part of me felt so ALONE. I couldn't put my finger on it at the time because, deep down, I had felt lonely all my life.

Oh, I can relate to that. I never felt I fitted in and always felt the odd one out...

That's it... We feel alone because we have disconnected from our core self, which also means we may not feel fully connected to the people around us. In addition, the people around us are also disconnected from their core selves, making it even trickier to find real, meaningful connections.

Kiddo, can I ask if you have any family or friends who are interested in personal growth and learning about themselves who can support you?

Some of my friends are into yoga and meditation, but that's it. Everyone else is just busy with ordinary life and work.

Why?

You see, it is typical for people like us to feel "the odd one out" because most people are just busy with everyday life. They are limited in their curiosity, and they will not start asking questions or want to do the work. This is why it can feel like a lonely place at the start of your self-discovery journey.

There's YOU who wants to know who you are and why you feel this way with all your questions. And then there are the people in your life who are quite frankly uninterested in learning about themselves.

Doesn't everyone want to know about themselves?

No, this is a big learning curve. You will find many people who will not share your passion for finding answers. They might be unhappy in themselves, but they still won't try to find a solution...

But that's mad – why wouldn't they?

Because they are not ready yet... Trust me... I've learned this the hard way – I thought I could take everyone with me on this journey, only to discover I couldn't. The truth is that people need to be ready and willing to learn and grow. We cannot make them... I am telling you this so you are prepared. You might even have people question why you want to learn about yourself. Most people don't understand why anyone would want to ask so many questions.

So, are you saying this is quite a lonely journey?

It can be in the beginning, but it doesn't have to be because many people like us are waking up. Asking questions, and you can connect with them when you know where to find them.

How do I find them?

You will connect with them by following the breadcrumbs. Follow your curiosity. By learning new things that interest you, you will meet people who share your interests and are also on their journey of discovering their core authentic selves.

What are these breadcrumbs you are talking about?

Oh, that could be a book, podcast, or presentation introducing you to a new teacher. Then you check out that teacher and listen to an interview with them in which they talk about a technique. Then, you look into that technique, and by doing so, you find a practitioner in your area who holds a session. So, you go and check this out. Then you meet local like-minded people and make friends. These friends will provide extra sources of inspiration. You will be amazed to find out that you are, in fact, NOT ALONE... You will discover that people have been on the journey of self-discovery for centuries. You will discover that there are many people ahead of you on the journey. You will discover an abundance of teachers, teachings, tools, techniques and modalities that can all help you on your journey. You will discover they all work similarly by letting go of the conditioning or stuck energy.

Oh, I had absolutely no idea.

That's OK; it's normal that we only experience what we focus on. I just wanted you to know that your tribe is out there, and until you find them, you will connect with people to help facilitate that journey. Some may only touch your life briefly; others may become firm friends and companions.

That sounds great...

Yes, it is...

But I hear a BUT coming...

Well, yes... I think I ought to tell you that by going on this journey of growth and self-discovery, you will grow and change.

I think I am aware of that…

So, what's the BUT?

The BUT comes with you growing and changing. The people you once felt close with might resonate less with you. They won't necessarily be interested in the same topics. So, as you meet new people, old friends might disappear because you no longer have things in common. This is another reason people are afraid of change. They want to keep everything the same, even if they are unhappy or unfulfilled.

As you grow and learn, you will see this more and more, and this is part of your learning to understand that not everyone will come with you on this journey. You may have to leave some people behind to find your happiness.

Why are you telling me this… it all sounded so lovely meeting new people with similar interests. But as a price, I have to leave some of my existing friends behind… it sounds selfish.

Ahh, that's the word I was waiting for

"SELFISH…"

YES, and you might hear that word from the people who don't understand the journey that you are on. They might call you "selfish" because, as you realise that you are significant and worthy, you start prioritising your needs and desires and putting them second. You will possibly get a kickback from them.

So, what's the answer?

The answer is – it's your choice.

You can choose to prioritise others over yourself and neglect what you want. Or you can prioritise what you want over what others want... Either way, you are selfish, or they are.

OK, I am playing devil's advocate here. There is a middle ground. You can be selfish, prioritise your needs and have healthy boundaries in place that let the people around you know what they can and can't expect from you.

This way, you can look after your needs while also creating healthy relationships with the people around you. The people who don't resonate with you anymore (as you change) will normally quietly disappear from your life, and you won't even notice because you have made many new friends who are way more on your wavelength.

That's good to know; thank you for warning me. I can see why change would scare some people. But I think it's a great opportunity to learn and meet more people like me.

Absolutely, and it's those new friends who understand you. Who will encourage you to continue to grow and stay on your journey.

I remember the first time I attended an event with people who were also interested in improving their lives. There was an openness and curiosity, and the energy in the room was so light and uplifting. I didn't know what "energy" was back then, but I could feel it. I knew I had found MY tribe...

Wow, that sounds amazing! So, how do I find my tribe, my community of people that resonate with me?

You consciously decide to go on this journey.

I knew I had been looking for something to fulfil me, but I could not decide what that was…

So, what did you do?

I listened to an intuitive thought that popped into my head that said:

"Don't rush anything. Give yourself ONE year to learn something new every day before committing to anything."

And did you listen to that inner voice?

Yes, I did!

As it was close to the end of the year, I decided to learn something new every day. I learned about meditation, hypnosis, NPL, and the universal laws. I learned about nutrition and healing. I listened to life coaches, inspirational teachers and practitioners. I followed the breadcrumbs until I discovered an alignment technique that helped me in my breakthrough.

So, you just knew…

When I discovered that "muscle testing" and using my body as a pendulum could help me unlock the answers within myself, I knew I had found what I was looking for.

And then what did you do?

I committed to consistently doing the work, and with the support of the coaches and fellow students in the community, I chipped away my layers. I began uncovering my true self. I discovered my passion for this work. I discovered my talents and my intuitive gifts. I discovered I could guide others on that journey.

Wow... and then what?

I decided to become a coach myself. Once I qualified, I continued learning and subsequently created my own approach called F.L.O.W. to FREEDOM, where I teach how to come in alignment with the seven CORE TRUTHS.

Ahhh, I can see now why you know so much...

So, have you discovered your highest purpose yet?

Yes, I have discovered my highest purpose thanks to the journey I have been on.

And, can I ask what it is?

Yes, you can, but haven't you guessed it yet?

How would I guess what YOUR purpose is?

My purpose is to remind people of their greatness and how they can strip back the layers of conditioning. My purpose is to guide and mentor those who want to find the answers within themselves and become their most authentic selves.

My purpose is to help others find clarity on their highest purpose.

My purpose is to:

- support those who want to improve their lives to feel happier.
- serve those who know they are here for a reason and want to make an impact in the world.
- teach how we can free ourselves from unwanted programming and conditioning by finding the answers within ourselves.
- mentor those who want to find more clarity on their message.
- guide those who struggle to gain more confidence to take action and make it happen.

Holy Moly... that's what we've been talking about the entire time.

What a coincidence!

I believe there are NO coincidences.

You and I were meant to meet. You had questions, and I had answers. This is how the universe works. Our conversation here may have been a breadcrumb for you that lets you discover your next stepping stone on your journey.

So, what should I do next?

OK, we are nearly complete. There is just KEY number, FOUR, and that is Clarity & Confidence.

CHAPTER 27

KEY FOUR:
CLARITY & CONFIDENCE

Right, tell me about clarity & confidence.

OK, remember I told you I gave myself a year to learn something new because I wasn't sure of my next steps, and I looked into many things until I had clarity?

Yes...

My best advice for the next part of the journey would be just to give things a go if they resonate. You may try something that looks exciting but turns out not so great. It will still be a stepping stone in the right direction. Likewise, anything you have tried right up to this point has brought you here. So, whatever it was, however good or mediocre, it got you right here.

Without it, we wouldn't have had this conversation, and you wouldn't know what you know now.

But what do I do with it?

OK, let me ask you a few questions... Have you discovered anything about yourself during our conversation?

Yes, I like asking questions and finding answers...

And have you learned anything?

Yes, I have the answers within myself, and there is a way to unlock them.

And has this shifted something in you?

Yes, I want to know more. I want to get started- I want to discover my purpose.

188

So, are you saying that what you heard gave you more clarity about what you want?

Yes, I guess it did. It's nice, after such a long time struggling to know there IS a way out of this. There is hope, and it's even normal to feel this way, and it is just a journey that I need to go on.

You mean a journey you WANT to go on?

Sorry, what did I say?

You said a journey you NEED to go on...

What's the difference?

Well, if you feel you "need to" do this – it's like you are being forced to do something. Nobody "needs to" go on the journey of self-discovery. Like everything - it's your choice. You should be clear about what you want. You can use your inner guidance and your sway at the beginning to decipher what is in alignment with your highest interest.

Do you mean I use the SWAY to check?

Yes, if you are not sure, you can ask your SWAY:

"Is it my highest interest... to do this course or read this book, etc?" You let your energy guide you. As you chip back the layers, your intuitive knowing will improve, your trust in yourself will increase, and eventually, you won't need to sway on it anymore.

So, can I use it to get clarity?

Yes, and that gives you confidence when you are unsure. Feel into what you come across – it is important that it resonates with your core self, and the sway can help you.

Pick the tools that resonate.

Choose the techniques that inspire you.

Decide which teacher you like best.

Check out the people who work with this coach.

Why?

It will give you an idea of the entire package. If the people who resonate with the coach and the approach or technique resonate with you, the rest might also do. They are the tribe. They can give you a sense of the vibe. They can give you confidence that you are in the right place.

So, are you saying to get clarity and confidence before committing?

Kiddo, as I said, you cannot get it wrong even if you decide to give something a go and it doesn't turn out the best thing you could have committed to – it is still a learning experience. I am saying, listen in and follow your heart as much as possible. If you don't have clarity, maybe just dip your toes in. Test things.

It's all good.

I see…

But do me one favour…

Yes?

When you get that absolute "knowing" feeling that something could be for you but comes at an unexpected time or in an unexpected way, please don't dismiss it!

Why would I dismiss it?

Because so often, we can be too much in our heads. We often THINK we know what the next logical step is, and it's easy to dismiss something that doesn't fit that idea.

Please be prepared that the right thing might come to you at a time when you least expect it. It may come to you in a different shape or form than what you thought would be your next step.

So, allow yourself to be open to a change in direction.

The universe doesn't deliver to you the opportunities that you think you "need". The universe gives you the opportunities that are right for you... Then it's your choice if you follow your head or your heart's impulse.

How do I know what my heart is telling me?

You will feel it in your energy as an intuitive "inner knowing" or a calling... You will know when something feels "just right", like a homecoming, a no-brainer or super exciting.

And remember, you can always double-check with your SWAY, and you are good to go.

Amazing – that's so cool! THANK YOU...

You are very welcome, and now, I am afraid it is time to say goodbye.

I hope you've enjoyed our conversation. I hope you got some clarity and new ideas on how you can move forward. I will give you just a few last words of advice:

Trust in yourself.

Believe in your greatness.

Remember that at the CORE of your being, YOU KNOW that you are:

SAFE, LOVED, WORTHY, SIGNIFICANT,

POWERFUL, ABUNDANT & FREE!

Go out there and connect with like-minded people.

Learn from the teachers that inspire you.

Find the answers within yourself.

Become the best version of yourself.

Discover your passion.

Live your highest potential and purpose.

And have fun doing so – that's the KEY.

And remember, YOU ARE THE PURPOSE!

Aww, I don't like saying goodbye, especially now that I want to learn more.

What if I want to learn more from YOU?

Ahh, Kiddo, it was an absolute pleasure meeting you. I am flattered that this conversation inspired you to take action and that you feel I could be the right teacher for you. You are welcome to check out my website for extra support & free resources at: www.UNLOCKyourANSWERS.com

I will!

THANK YOU so much for your time and teachings today.

Do you know what?

What?

I think you could write this down and inspire others. There must be lots of people like ME who feel a bit lost...

You really are full of surprises! I like the idea of inspiring others to find hope and discover a way out.

Guaranteed...

You know what? I might do that. I will recall our conversation and write it all down.

Excellent, I am looking forward to getting a copy.

You will...

Oh, one last thing before we go...

Yes?

I think: "YOU ARE THE PURPOSE"

would make a great name for a book.

Thank you, Kiddo

I will keep it in mind...

X

About the Author

Kat Catlin is an Intuitive Alignment Coach & Teacher. From a young age, she was curious about what "makes us tick" and what the meaning of life is.

Her journey into personal growth and self-help began when she found herself disempowered and LOST in herself. Not knowing her purpose, she decided "something had to change". She began asking questions and found answers. She discovered the reason she felt unhappy, frustrated and out of alignment were subconscious, limiting beliefs she held about herself. She also discovered a way to unlock the answers within herself and shift these limiting beliefs at the root cause level.

Understanding that every one of us is unique and complex because we are deeply conditioned and programmed, Kat decided to look for patterns. This led her to identify seven CORE TUTHS and LIMITING BELIEFS most of us carry, which can be responsible for our unwanted triggers, patterns and negative emotions.

Kat is passionate about teaching clients how to let go of their limiting stories and align with their true authentic selves so they can step back into their power, discover their life purpose and live their highest potential.

Additional Resources & Support

If the content in this book has brought up questions, you would like to learn more or feel inspired to take action to unlock your unique answers. Please check our website for more information and how to get started...

Visit:

www.UNLOCKyourANSWERS.com

Where you can access:

*Free Resources

*Video Tutorials

*How to Guides

*Contact Details

*Coaching Offers

*Courses Availability

*Info on how to join our vibrant Community

We are looking forward to seeing you there.

x

Milton Keynes UK
Ingram Content Group UK Ltd.
UKHW020143051123
431882UK00011B/122